TAMSIN WESTHORPE

Grasping the Nettle

Tales from a

MODERN COUNTRY GARDENER

with illustrations by
Rosalie Herrera

ORPHANS
publishing

Tamsin would like to thank her editor Debbie Hatfield,
illustrator Rosalie Herrera and all at Orphans Publishing
for making this experience such fun. Great teamwork!

First published in Great Britain in 2022 by
Orphans Publishing
www.orphanspublishing.co.uk

Text copyright © Tamsin Westhorpe, 2022
Illustrations copyright © Rosalie Herrera, 2022

A Cataloguing in Publication record for this book is available from the
British Library.

Hardback ISBN: 978-1-903-36051-4

Printed and bound by Clays Ltd., Elcograf, S.p. A.

To my darling boy Herbie.
You are my biggest achievement.
Follow your dreams.
With love Mamma Mia x

Contents

Introduction
or
Which Side of the Fence Do You Belong?

When did you last stop and think about how much things have changed during your lifetime? Looking around me now, and thinking back to the experiences of my childhood, it's apparent that the world has evolved beyond recognition. Nothing is exempt from the passing of time and fashions, not even the natural world of trees and plants and the way we garden. Allow me to take you back in time...

I was born in the summer of 1972, when the miners were on strike and Chuck Berry was in the charts with 'My Ding-a-Ling'. Cheese and pineapple skewered on cocktail sticks was considered a delicacy, washed down by bottles of Blue Nun and tables adorned with centrepieces of Blue Moon roses (despite the fact that both sound like titles of risqué erotic movies). Polyester was the must-have material of the day, brown was in for interiors and spider plants in macramé hangers and bottle gardens were all the rage.

Outdoors, however, colour was king. Perhaps gardening in the seventies was inspired by the outrageous shades and styles of the outfits of ABBA, who formed the year I was born. Regimented rows of orange marigolds flanked by red begonias against a backdrop of pink or yellow roses was the norm. Google images of gardens from that era and you'll think you're on a drug-induced trip or that you've jumped into *The Magic Roundabout* (for those that are too young to remember, this was a rather trippy children's cartoon series of yesteryear). Back then, our most respected gardening experts wore a tie or smoked a pipe – of course, they were all men. Compare this to the gentle swathes of meadow-style planting and subtle colour theming we favour in our gardens today, a lot of it inspired by female landscape designers, and the contrast couldn't be greater. Like music, fashion and food, gardening has changed, and will continue to do so. The ideas of today will be frowned upon in the future, just like we raise our own eyebrows at the past – it's as inevitable as the fact that we will all turn into our parents. (I've already joined my mother on the church council, something I vowed I would never do!) There is one thing that I'm confident won't ever change: that gardening and plants make a difference to everyone's lives, giving us memories, providing life-changing experiences and helping us to become who we are. Whether you're a gardener or non-gardener, and whether you choose to get your hands dirty or not, absolutely everyone is influenced by plants in one way or another.

If my memory serves me correctly, life seemed far less complicated in the 1970s. It was the era of Tom and Barbara in *The Good Life*, when the focus was on make-do-and-mend and family fun. My early childhood coincided with a time when hand-me-down clothes were acceptable attire and jumble sales were an important social and shopping event. Many of us over a certain age will recall our parents putting one or more of our old toys into such a sale. It was only when you saw your doll or stuffed animal drowning under a sea of old – and often smelly – shirts and scarves that you realised how much Teddy, Cindy or (in my case) Ken meant to you. Of course, you'd end up buying it back yourself. Acquiring a school friend's second-hand jumper from a jumble sale came with no side-swiping comments as I'm sure it might today. If our clothes weren't second-hand, they were hand-made. I recall spending many happy hours looking through patterns in the fabric shop as a child. My taste was rather flamboyant in those days, with rah-rah skirts being my favourite (the icing on those outfits was a pair of luminous legwarmers). Watching the shopkeeper roll out my chosen fabric on the giant table gave me just the best feeling and having it cut to length with enormous serrated scissors produced the most wonderful sound. When so much thought has gone into an outfit, you want to keep it forever. When it's finally outgrown you might hand it down to a sibling or perhaps keep it to make it into a cushion – you feel connected to its very being. Back then, we seemed to accept that things took time: the words 'instant' or 'quick fix' were almost never spoken. Patience is the quintessential quality of a gardener – you can't speed up the passing of time needed for plants to thrive.

Looking back now, I wonder if we've lost some of that connection with time and the natural world since the appearance of social media and other modern trappings. Yes, online platforms are a great way of sharing ideas and knowledge, which I'm absolutely all for, but are we now so set on showing ourselves in a good light that we've forgotten how to appreciate an apple with a perfectly formed maggot hole or the allotment shed with a pleasingly cracked window pane? A garden – and a life, for that matter – with flaws is often one filled with much fun and adventure. The best gardens you come across in life aren't necessarily the ones with perfect colour, texture and form; instead they're the ones that have been lived in and loved. Somewhere along the way, it seems to me that we have added a huge amount of stress, speed, competition and materialistic desire into the mix and forgotten the basics. When did we all suddenly need to have every cushion on the sofa artfully curated? What happened to homes and gardens filled with an eclectic bunch of favourite items? Why does anyone need a set of matching mugs anyway? Is it this desire to live in a perfectly colour-themed world that has led to things being thrown out rather than repurposed, recycled or re-loved? Perhaps I feel this keenly because I've never managed to create a garden that seamlessly flows or a home that is a comfortable collection of complimentary tones – could I be jealous of those that have? My problem, though, isn't that I don't have a good eye for colour, it's that I get attached to items from the past and can't let them go. I like my garden and my home to not simply be full of things that I bought from an anonymous garden centre or home store to fulfil my desire to follow the latest trends. I want places packed with possessions and plants that tell stories. After all, I'd far rather spend my days on Barbara and Tom's side of the fence than on Margo and Jerry's – wouldn't you?

To remind you of what life used to be like, before it was Instagrammable and always shown in soft focus, I want to take you back to simpler days. I'll explore how things have changed in horticulture since then with some stories from my life that I hope will entertain you as well as inform. Moving from the comfort of an idyllic childhood into adulthood was a challenge for me, as it is for many people. Finding horticulture made that transition more agreeable. If I'd been a follower of fashion back then, I might now be a secretary or teacher and not a gardener. But I took a different path, and if I had my time again, I wouldn't choose any other career. It hasn't always been the easiest ride or the most financially rewarding but it has helped me to stay connected to my past and grow at the same time. The jobs and life experiences that mould you and give you knowledge are often those that aren't glamorous or high-flying. My life in gardening has been varied, with both successes and failures. It's these downs as well as ups that form your character. I was often mucky, sometimes extremely cold and exhausted but ultimately happy. Horticulture has given me so much and been so fulfilling that I wanted to share a few of my stories in the hope of making others look at gardening in a very different light. Join me as I revisit how gardening has provided me with love, friendship and lots of laughter. Pull on your steel toe-capped boots and let's dig in!

Daisy Petals and Dandelion Clocks

My early childhood was spent mostly outside, by all accounts. My parents weren't avid gardeners, but they certainly made sure that my sisters and I made our fair share of mud pies. They were far too busy to wet wipe us clean or worry about us climbing trees or eating the odd worm. There were always hundreds of pairs of welly boots by our back door – more time was spent outside than in. When we were corralled inside, life was a tapestry of turning the lights off after leaving a room, eating everything on your plate and sharing your siblings' bath water – being the middle sister, I'm not sure I ever got totally clean. My mother always had chickens in the back of the car – yes, really, the car! She was a fanatical poultry breeder, which might explain why our bath water was always dirty. The house wasn't full of seed trays in spring, as mine is now, but instead incubators with hatching chicks all over the place. There were makeshift little chicken runs lined with sheets of newspaper in nearly every room and the tweets of fluffy yellow chicks were the music of the household. As a child my preferred diet was chocolate buttons, egg sandwiches and offal of any kind and I would much rather eat in the garden than at a table. If the weather was inclement and I was summoned inside by my parents, I would sometimes choose to eat under the table and listen to the family conversation going on over my head. You'll be glad to hear that I have now expanded my culinary choices somewhat and will sit at a table without stamping my feet first.

Soon enough, it was time to follow my older sister to school. What I remember of this early education was all rather wonderful – apart from the constant nagging to drink warm milk, eat my lunch and learn my times tables. Those little glass milk bottles that I once tried so hard to avoid are now something I avidly hunt for in antique shops, as they make perfect vases for sweet peas. Back then, I took the view that life was far too interesting to waste time eating or drinking. Now, of course, I would do pretty much anything to be served up a school meal during my working day as a gardener.

My primary school was rather quaintly situated in a village with a local shop, church and village green. It was the sort of place that you would expect to see in a Miss Marple movie: traffic passed through slowly, the vicar was always on hand and villagers all doffed their caps on passing each other. The green was where we learnt to dance around a Maypole and play rounders, both of which involved wearing little black pumps, a white vest and shorts (I haven't been seen in shorts since). We would often walk through the village and surrounding fields and woods as part of our lessons. I have a vivid memory of running along a footpath in summer that took us up a steep hill through the main artery of a cornfield. Think of the scene at the beginning and end of the television series of *Little House on the Prairie* – that is exactly how I felt, and I even had the plaited pigtails and elasticated homemade skirt to complete the picture. Life was a hop, skip and jump with insects, petals and fluffy clouds all thrown in for good measure. This was before the time of Ofsted, in the days when learning about our natural surroundings was a priority and children were allowed to play conkers and make mud pies (and even attempt to eat them) at break times. When we were told to wash our hands before lunch we really needed to. The great thing about nature walks is suddenly everyone in the class is on an even keel. No one is top of the set and maths, English and art can be woven in unnoticed. Counting petals on a daisy, telling the time by a dandelion clock, or seeing how many acorns we could collect was a far better way to learn numbers than with an abacus. (Here is where I confess that I bought an abacus for my son's nursery almost as soon as he was born. I suppose I was hoping that the presence of these magical wooden beads would automatically make him a mathematician. It didn't work.)

Yes, primary school was great for me apart from the odd lack of judgment on my part. My weekends at home were often spent collecting snails and other creepy crawlies. Gerald Durrell and I would've been the greatest of friends. One Monday morning, I decided to put a few of my slippery pets into a sandwich box and then tip them as a gift into my schoolteacher's top desk drawer. When she opened it to pull out the chalk, I can recall her scream as if it were yesterday. Obviously, I was reprimanded for this action but I couldn't quite understand why she wouldn't want snails all over her paperwork. I'd spent many happy hours watching my pets making their way around the mini garden I had created for them in a Fox's biscuit tin that lived under my bed. How could they fail to entertain? I feel slightly different about snails now, but at that stage in my life, I didn't see the negative side of having them in the garden. To me, they were my friends. I enjoyed hunting them down to admire and care for them. I still rather like the fact that they can retreat into a shell when danger approaches – how wonderful to carry something around that you can quickly hide in whenever you choose.

Anyway, along with egging my friend on to see how far he could stick a wax crayon up his nose whilst we were supposed to be making Easter bunnies, this was my sum of primary school mishaps. The wax crayon led to an ambulance arriving, followed by my friend's concerned mother, and my angry mother following not that far behind. The only other time I have seen my mother so cross was at a garden centre. She is a good gardener but not a fanatical one, poultry being her passion instead. This didn't stop her from taking us on very regular, almost weekly trips to the garden centre after school. I recall this particular visit clearly, as I had accepted a piece of bubble gum from a kid I was keen to impress at school and was trying to inconspicuously chew it as we wandered the aisles past hyacinth bulbs and bird feed. My sisters and I were banned from eating such devilish stuff and I almost felt as rebellious as I would if I were following my mother through the store with a cigarette hanging out of my mouth. Once the strawberry flavour had passed, I spat the gum into my hand and gripped it tightly. I had intended to drop it into a bin without my mother noticing. But by the time I spotted a bin, the gum was stuck between my fingers and, in my attempts to rectify that, to my other hand as well. I was in one big sticky mess. Of course, my mother noticed and was furious. My penance was that I had to forgo the rocket ice lolly that my sisters got to choose from the garden centre freezer. There was no chance of me holding a lolly with my fingers stuck together. After such a traumatic attempt to be cool, I was destined to toe the line for the rest of my school life. I wasn't cut out to be a gum-chewing rebel. In fact, as a teenager I went on to work at the garden centre my mother loved so dearly. It was here that I learnt many plant names, mastered the art of pricing up Christmas baubles, stood up endless plants on windy days, carried Christmas trees to people's cars and, on occasion, assisted our most exciting customer – Penelope Keith. Imagine my thrill when I spotted Margo amongst the magnolias. Definitely a high point of my career.

Back at primary school, the rest of my days were largely spent pulling apart ears of corn, peeling the bark off sticks and crushing rose petals to make perfume. I didn't have to be taught about spring, summer, autumn and winter as a theoretical lesson – my friends and I were part of each season. We lived and breathed the different sights and smells – although taking in the perfume that nature provides is only possible when you don't have a wax crayon shoved up your nose! Meanwhile, my childhood interest in creating a menagerie in my bedroom was accompanied by my passion for growing plants from seed and digging up small tree seedlings.

On one birthday (probably my tenth) I asked my parents for a greenhouse. They presented me with a terrarium. It was lovely but certainly not what I had been hoping for – my plan was to grow on a larger scale. I'd spotted an old hard standing in the garden where a shed once stood. Surely building a greenhouse there would be a simple matter? Being the wonderful parents that they are, they somehow procured an old greenhouse. Anyone that has tried to rebuild a second-hand greenhouse will know how hard they are to reconstruct, so this was a gesture of serious love. My father persevered for I dread to think how many hours or even days. It was so worth it for me, though – and for my mother. The many pots of seedlings that I would grow in old yoghurt pots and place in her airing cupboard amongst the clean white sheet now had a more suitable home. My only disappointment was that my budgerigar, Valentine, wasn't allowed to live in my glass palace. I'd hoped he could fly around amongst the tomato plants, but my parents rightly insisted that he would get too hot. Unfortunately for Valentine, with my attention firmly on activities in the greenhouse I'm afraid that he didn't get the consideration he deserved. It wasn't long before my mother had given him to the milkman. About a week after he had moved into his new home, I noticed the empty aviary and ran into the house crying 'My Valentine has gone!' This wasn't the last time I would say these words in my life, I can assure you! I had learnt the hard way that animals and plants need constant attention, or they would die or be seen heading off into the distance on the milk float.

Spur Hill Avenue

Every summer, my parents would take my sisters and I to paradise by the sea. The car would be loaded up with air beds, tents, buckets and spades. Our destination wasn't a swanky beachside hotel – oh, no, to me it was far better than that. We would stay with my great aunt in her very damp ground floor flat at Spur Hill Avenue in Poole, Dorset.

In its heyday, the house in which Auntie Margie had her flat would have been rather grand. Panels of stained glass bedecked the front door, the hall was tiled beautifully, it had impressively high ceilings and the large windows had windowsills deep enough to sit on. Apart from splitting the house into three flats, it was as if time had stood still. Auntie Margie was every bit as glamorous as the house. The bright light in the family who added that touch of glamour, she was poor as a church mouse but oozed style. She belonged in a black and white movie and had the wit and charm to always be the leading lady. Much of her life had been spent working for Helena Rubenstein, selling and demonstrating the art of applying make-up. I don't recall ever seeing her without lipstick – her cigarette butts were all ringed with her trademark circle of red lippy. To me she was a Hollywood movie star. She had a better grasp on life than anyone else I've ever met – she had really lived. She taught me three very important lessons in life, all of which I have followed. Always paint your toenails, never wear elasticated leggings (not becoming on any lady) and never get involved with a Sagittarian man (I'll spare you the details, but I tried it once and she was quite right).

I can't imagine what an imposition and shock it must have been having our family arrive en masse every summer. Auntie Margie seemed to delight at our arrival, however. The flat was rarely heated until guests arrived, and I clearly recall steam rising from the mattress in the spare room as she attempted to hastily dry it out with fan heaters. It was as if every piece of furniture in the flat had had three lifetimes; each glass, ornament and lampshade had a thousand stories to tell. The bath tap would choke when turned on; in contrast, the kitchen tap would scream. These quirks all added to the experience of the stay. Although her belongings were very much of the past (some of the tins in the kitchen cupboard were years out of date and her perfume was so old I suspect it had turned to pure alcohol), Auntie Margie was so excited by the future. She tolerated our dreadful music and far from stylish fashion choices. She was accepting of us all (as long as we stuck to her three rules). I could just tell that she wanted us to grab life by the cut-glass crystal balls!

If the weather allowed, my sisters and I would fight to be the one who would sleep in the one-man tent in the garden. This tent was a classic. My grandmother had saved up the coupons on the back of her McDougall's flour packets to buy it. It was a bright green-blue, and when inside on a sunny day the light was dreamy. I can't say it was water-tight! I'm pretty sure I have knickers that would be more weatherproof than that tent, but we were young enough not to care about comfort.

At first glance, the garden was nothing to write home about. Average size, lawn, shed, coal bunker, a fence on two sides and a row of conifers on the other. My aunt's planting palette was basic and reliable. Runner beans, spinach, nasturtiums and a passionflower were almost the only inhabitants. Looking back, I realise that she was the ultimate make-do and mend gardener. The passionflower that romped along the back fence was hitched up with old tights, whilst buckets, broken teapots and even old shoes were planted with her beloved nasturtiums. You took your life into your own hands when you sat in one of the old deck chairs – would this be the one to collapse? The shed was home to an array of ancient tools, most without handles and an electric mower that should have been condemned. Auntie Margie would mow the lawn in stages, holding the electric cable in one hand and a cigarette in the other.

Although it was far from designed, this plot was my aunt's special place. And through the eyes of a child, it had it all. It was a place people felt welcome and happy to behave in any way they liked. There were no rules, and you were never told to "get out of the border". We would play badminton over the washing line and eat every meal we possibly could under the sun that shone on Spur Hill Avenue. The only part of the garden that was gloomy was the back passage that ran between her house and next door. This was a classic north-facing passageway where an antique gnome lived. We still have that gnome – he's a family heirloom.

You might wonder why I am reminiscing about this very ordinary garden. I think it is only now, as I begin to write this book, that I realise what an impact it had on me as a gardener. Aunt Margie's garden wasn't about snazzy varieties and planned displays. It was simply a home; a place to enjoy with family. Growing up, some of my other relatives had rather smart formal gardens but this was an escape from law, order and pretence. This was a holiday.

Working Hands and False Teeth

"When did you know that you were going to become a gardener?"

Every journalist who interviews someone who professionally leans on the handle of a spade will ask this predictable question. The most common answer given, in my experience, is that they were inspired by 'gardening grandparents' or they took to gardening after a tough time at school and it saved them from going off the rails. When I ask myself the same thing, I can't be sure of the exact moment my own fingers started to turn green and I began to peer into every flower I passed. I can't claim that horticulture saved me from turning into someone that my parents would be ashamed of, but I can claim that it has given me a career that fits and suits me. Gardening and I rub along nicely together, and I've never had to pretend to be anything I'm not. After briefly trying a few other career options I can confidently say that horticulture is my world and my happy place. Thank the Lord we found each other.

I'm not convinced that there is always one lightbulb moment when your calling as a career gardener dawns on you. I suspect it might be more likely to happen to people a decade or so down another path, working hard at something they dislike. I can see how suddenly catching a glimpse of a flowering cherry from the office or factory window might see you abandoning your post and running towards that vision of gorgeousness, heading for a new life. Instead, I think finding the right career is a little like choosing a wedding dress. Not every bride has that feeling when they believe they have become the most beautiful woman in the world. I spotted my wedding dress in the window of a bridal shop whilst waiting at the traffic lights. It was pink – yes, I adored it, but I can't claim that it made me cry, or feel like Cinderella in her glass slippers. I just knew that it was right for me and I wasn't even tempted to try anything else on.

If forced to pin point the moment I chose my career, it might have been way back in the mid 1980s, when I was a young teenager. Picture this. A skinny girl, last to hit puberty in her class – or possibly the school – with ears that no girl would be proud of (My mother would try to hide my ears by pulling my hair over them before tying a pigtail. This made matters far worse, as it was the preferred hairstyle of our physics teacher. The result was that everyone in my class always assumed I was her love child!). I was a day pupil at a boarding school – it was a place of draughty halls, heavy doors and beauty everywhere. There were girls in my year group who had a glow and a confidence that I envied and admired. They were the dahlias of the border; I was the willow herb.

I wasn't an unhappy child – far from it. My parents were more than amazing but they couldn't protect me from the sharp tongues of my peers. Mind you, I didn't help myself. To add to the ears and the pigtails, if I could, I'd keep my long coat on all day and I would run everywhere. I'm not sure if I was running away from life or racing into it with excitement – a bit of both, I suspect. My hobbies included keeping grass snakes under my bed and breeding white mice that I would periodically release at school. At one point I had a tank for my grass snakes and a cage for my mice placed next to each other on the top of my wardrobe. Cruel, really, when you consider that the snakes would probably have enjoyed snacking on the mice – temptation for the snakes, terror for the rodents. One of my proudest moments came when a rumour started flying around that a white mouse had been spotted in the school chapel. I had released said mouse in this house of God during a boring singing practice. I loved the idea of it nibbling the hymn books and making a nest in a kneeler. If a mouse died in my care at home, I would take it to school in my coat pocket and ceremoniously cremate it in the school wood at breaktime. I recall asking a teacher if I could borrow a box of matches and she happily gave me one with no questions asked. Just wonderful. Imagine the headline – 'Girl Sets Fire to School Woods Cremating Pet Mouse'. In hindsight, she obviously knew I wasn't the type of pupil who was going to light up a cigarette. I wasn't that cool.

Like many, I struggled with the concept of learning and listening. After all, who needs to know how fast light travels, what a molecule is made up of or why X equals Y? My primary focus was on finding love. Hours were spent daydreaming about the boys in the class – every week a different one would catch my attention. The interest was never returned. Until one day there was a ray of hope…

Biology class, 1983. The task was to dissect a pig's heart. Now this was something I could see the point of. I'd run a mile from blood now but in those days, the gorier the better. The heart was real, not some figures or equations on a board but something with a purpose (well, it was before the pig died!). As I held my scalpel over the heart, I turned to see how the boy next to me was going to cut his. Copying was something that got me through school (I'm not proud of it, but it saved me on more than one occasion). I can recall my classmate's hands to this day. He had a thumbnail that looked as if it belonged to an older man, someone who had worked physically hard. Under the nail was soil. To most girls, his hands would have been disgusting, but not to me. They fascinated me. I moved my eyes further up his body (not down, don't panic!). He wasn't a boy of classic good looks. He was someone who could possibly, at an outside chance, be in my league. On closer inspection, I noticed that he had a false front tooth. What joy to find someone with a fault to such a degree – there was no chance he could turn me down now, surely? Over the next few weeks, we began to talk, not much but enough to make my heart flutter (not something that the pig's heart could do any longer). It was enough to make me ditch the vest that my mother made me wear every day. No one apart from my sisters and I wore vests and we would remove them on the walk to school as soon as our house was out of sight. Now as a gardener I can't get enough of these undergarments (my mother was right, as always) but at the time wearing a vest was about as uncool as you could get.

The boy's conversation was largely about his passion for trees and his friendship with his pet rat. I was hooked. Being the proud owner of a mini greenhouse that was home to a successful crop of tomatoes, I dropped in mentions of my horticultural prowess. After all, with the tomato being commonly known as the love apple, I thought this would work its magic. Alas, this was not enough for him to slip a note into my pocket (At my school it was customary for boys to write you a little note asking you out, but my pockets remained empty apart from the odd seed pod I'd collected from the school grounds).

It was this toothless wonder that put the idea into my head that gardening might be a good place to head if my fancy was for a man with working hands and false teeth. Unlike the other girls I wasn't for a man in a uniform. Richard Gere never did it for me. I was looking for someone rough around the edges who had that all-important soil under their nails and a passion for the natural world. Gardening was now definitely on my list of career possibilities.

In my final year at school, I was asked what career path I hoped to take. When I suggested gardening, I was offered work experience with a beautician. Perhaps it was the closest to pruning they could get. A day spent with immaculately made-up girls, reclining beds, moisturiser, joss sticks, the unbearable scent of nail polish and a backing track of whale sounds confirmed that this wasn't for me. I was an awkward teenager with buck teeth who owned just one ghastly sky-blue eye shadow palette and an eye liner given to me by Father Christmas in my early teens. The day would've been far better spent if the beauticians had given me a much-needed makeover, rather than a series of demonstrations on removing unwanted body hair. Until that day, I'd had no idea that having hot wax deliberately put onto your body was a thing – and that people were prepared to pay for the pleasure of having their hairs ripped out. I'm thankful that I was spared a life of massaging strangers, and plucking and waxing the unthinkable. It's only now I'm much older that I realise how essential the work of a beautician is – now I wouldn't be without them; the older I get, the more often I use their pruning services.

Having not taken to the beauty profession, on leaving school my parents decided to send me on a secretarial course. They were desperate to find a box for me to fit in. It was a crash course where you learnt to type in a week. Except that I didn't. I hated it and never completed the course. The thought of spending my life behind a desk in an office filled me with fear and dread. In hindsight, I wish I had paid more attention. As a garden writer, typing is a handy skill. At the time, though, I rejoiced on the day that I took the outfit my mother had bought me for the typing course to the charity shop. It was a dark green pair of culottes (sort of long shorts that appeared to be a skirt), coupled with a ghastly yellow and green shirt – I looked like I had been dressed by an ancient, spinster aunt, certainly not like Aunt Margie. It was mortifyingly dreadful. My mother usually has a great eye for fashion but on this occasion her style radar had run out of batteries.

As a result of my failed attempts at being a beauty therapist and a secretary – both classic female career options – I knew instinctively that I wasn't destined to follow any more obvious paths. I was going to steer well clear of anything that involved wearing a shirt that made me look like an MP or eyeshadow of any colour. At the time, of course, I showed no appreciation of the efforts my parents went to. They were just trying their best to find me a career where I would thrive. I was lucky to have parents who were in pursuit of my happiness and nothing else. Now, as the mother of a teenager myself, I understand the desperation a parent feels to help their child find happiness. It's really all that matters.

My suspicion is that I had made my mind up about being a gardener a few years before the trials and tribulations of work experience, back when I was discovering the delight of dirty fingernails on a boy. Back in the 1980s, gardening wasn't something that seemed a viable option for a girl, and even though I loved my plants I wasn't very sure how you could make a living in this field, so I was open to trying other ideas. To be perfectly honest, I suppose I hoped that I would marry someone who would support me financially and I'd have hours of free time to tend my garden. After reading *Pride and Prejudice* I was convinced that every girl would get the chance to be Elizabeth Bennet – my Mr Darcy would doubtlessly ensure that I could spend my time tending the cutting garden! I lived in my own little world. But I would soon need to make my way in the wider world all by myself.

Fly Me to the Moon

My plan after leaving school was to become a sculptor. Working with clay was one of the few things I had connected with at school as a teenager, and I had visions of myself as a modern-day Michelangelo, spending days massaging this silky-smooth substance to create magical outdoor features for gardens. My studio would be in the countryside, a place where models would lounge on chaises longue or lie on the lawn whilst I peered at them over my half glasses or from under a giant floppy summer hat. The aim was to recreate an exact image of my subject with my sculpting tools. In my imagination, my studio floor would be splattered with clay and so would I. The shelves would be filled with vases of seasonal flowers and old paintbrushes and the air full of the summer perfumes from the garden. Birdsong would be the soundtrack to my days. This romantic vision was more suited to a nineteenth-century lifestyle than the realities of the 1980s fast-paced pop culture. I often suspect I was born in the wrong era.

The only part of this idiotic childhood dream that has come true is that I did succeed in finding a career that put mud under my fingernails. The real connection between working with clay and gardening only became obvious to me decades later. Today I might not be crafting horses or naked bodies out of clay (my specialities at school), but I am creating art by growing plants in this medium. Most of my gardening life has been spent nurturing plants in Herefordshire's rich red clay soil. I have yet to find reason to combine gardening with nude models but I'm working on it. Leave that one with me.

To accomplish my sculptural dreams, I started art college. The truth is that I wasn't ready to be in that environment at sixteen years old. After trying to fit in with the 'arty types' for a few months, with no sign of working with clay on the timetable, I realised that it just wasn't for me. I had attempted to create an artistic character for myself by making my own clothes under the assumption that unique pieces of fashion would give me a head start. Many of these clothes were subsequently taken from my wardrobe by my grandmother to dress scarecrows, which tells you all you need to know about them!

My determination to draw things that looked like a real object also didn't go down well with the tutors. It seemed that they were looking for ground-breakers – movers and shakers who drew things that might be part of a cheese- and wine-induced nightmare, rather than the wildflowers I had admired on my country walk. It appeared to me that to be a successful artist you were required to have a slightly tortured look and a desire to shock, to throw out the rule book. I wasn't prepared to go to the lengths that Vincent van Gogh did to make a name for himself, so instead of removing an ear I decided to impress my tutor with a pencil drawing of a chicken carcass. I had wrongly assumed that presenting him with the remains of an animal was about as left-field as you could get and surely would result in high praise. It wasn't the best way to win over a vegetarian tutor! Adding to my bad feelings about art college I had a very unfortunate incident with a Bunsen burner. Whilst attempting to make jewellery I flicked my very long hair in a flirty manner in an attempt to impress a very attractive male student working opposite me. My locks caught fire. He leapt across the room, removed his jumper and threw it over my head to put out the flames. I was so enthralled by the hero in motion that the hideous smell of burning hair passed me by. So, yes, I got his attention but all for the wrong reasons. He avoided me thereafter. That was the final straw. Me and my homemade wardrobe just didn't fit into the art world.

I am now thankful for this brief episode as a failing artist as it was the final push towards my horticultural destiny. Now as the mother of a sixteen-year-old myself, I realise what a problem I was to my parents. What do you do with the quirky middle child who has dropped out of college? Brilliantly, my parents found me work at a relative's plant nursery. It was perfect. I had absolutely no desire to move on and up. But just when I thought I had found my happy place, I discovered a plan to send me off to another college, this time a horticultural one. Was there no escaping education?

I hadn't enjoyed the academic side of school, so my plan was to get in and out of horticultural college as quickly as possible. The thought of sitting at a desk, taking notes and doing exams was just hideous to me. To fulfil my quick exit strategy, I signed up for the shortest possible course on offer. I was to study Interior

Landscaping. What on earth is that, you might well ask? To be honest, I wasn't altogether sure myself.

After a few weeks, I realised that I had by chance fallen upon something rather wonderful. The course was practical and used my artistic skills. Back then, the world was on a health kick that involved legwarmers, leotards and peace lilies. Fitness experts were leaping around television studios in Lycra, the craze for aerobics was in full swing and the desire to stay healthy was very much on the agenda. Everyone was obsessed by keeping fit and healthy at home and at work – women's magazines featured models carrying a Filofax and styled with a Farrah Fawcett flick and curl. This made houseplants the obvious match for the health conscious. If you thought the excitement over houseplants was a new phenomenon in the last few years, then I'm here to tell you that it most certainly isn't. Rewind to the late eighties and early nineties and indoor foliage was fabulous and in fashion. Part of the nation's newfound health kick was to install houseplants into public spaces across the land for their oxygenating properties. Nearly every office block and hotel foyer had at least one ficus or diffenbachia. This trend for interior foliage and flowers coincided with a study by NASA (The National Aeronautics and Space Administration) on how houseplants cleaned our air. We were rocketing into a new era and the sky was the limit. I was going to be amongst a group of students who would be the first to study this new craze full-time. Interior Landscaping was such a flexible career choice offering part time, full time and entrepreneurial opportunities. I might not have been destined to be a mover and shaker in the art world, but I was about to become an astronaut of the gardening world! Having never been at the forefront of anything fashionable I was suddenly engaged and ready to star jump into this ground-breaking course. Had I struck gold?

The curriculum included houseplant care, some floristry and designing installations with interior plants for hotels, shopping centres and offices. The other students that joined me on this mission to Mars were an eclectic mix – some were career changers wanting to be their own boss, others failed A level students and then there were people like me, who didn't quite know how we'd ended up there but were just happy to be working with plants. Whilst studying the houseplants and their care at college, I remained blissfully unaware of the realities of the job. But within the course was a practical placement, which was when it hit home. Our days would be spent carrying watering cans up and down office stairs and cleaning nicotine off houseplant leaves with a damp cloth. Oh yes, and politely asking Lois Lane and Clark Kent lookalikes not to use the planters in the office as a place to pour coffee dregs! During my placement I quickly learned that this job was a little like being an air hostess and nothing like being an astronaut. You had a trolley and a uniform and although your job was mainly mundane you would suddenly have to step up and save a life at a moment's notice. Fortunately for me it was the life of a plant and not a person. I can also confirm that although I have been gardening outside for many years since, I have never been so dirty in all my life as I was then. Dust is a far worse an evil than soil. Mix dust with nicotine and stale coffee and you have the perfect filth. At the end of some days my hair would smell worse than when it was on fire under that Bunsen burner!

This placement allowed me to see the behind-the-scenes workings of large swanky offices and the kitchens of big hotels and restaurants. Let's face it – at the time I was adamant I was never going to be sitting behind a desk in an office, so it was an interesting insight. Back then, giant computers and fax machines the size of small skips filled the offices. Open plan was the new big thing but many workers hid behind blue desk screens whilst others made sure everyone could see their every move and enjoy the show they put on by glamorously swinging around in their swivel chairs. Their sharp suits and shoulder pads were a strong contrast to our polo shirts – mind you, when you think about it, the polo shirt has never become unfashionable whilst I suspect many look back at their shoulder-pad-wearing days with horror. The concept of power dressing certainly passed me by and for that I am very grateful.

Our base in large offices, hotels and shopping centres was often the windowless broom cupboard and the conundrum of the day was where to find a tap that the watering can would fit under. There were also many other challenging moments; for instance, when should we or shouldn't we enter a room to tend a plant? Picture this – a board meeting with very smartly dressed business people is ongoing but through the glass windows you can see that your beloved ficus needs its fortnightly drink or it's going to die. The plight of the plant has not been noticed by anyone but you. Life and death is in your hands! A particular kind of glance over the glasses from an office manager through the glass panel in the door could always stop me entering with my trolley – to me that remains a definite sign of 'Enter At Your Peril'. Repotting a six-foot dracaena in the office of a top executive without dropping any compost on the carpet tiles is another challenge, let me tell you. We couldn't use a vacuum cleaner as it would have disturbed the office folk, so I got very handy with a dustpan and brush. I think that a module in moving swiftly whilst carrying an unwieldy bag of compost or a spiky giant yucca should be added to interior landscaping courses. It would've been handy to have the skills to move through an office without being noticed. A few classes with the nimble-footed Anton du Beke might have helped us quick step out of tricky situations.

My time as an interior landscaper was also my first experience of the world of coffee. My family are tea drinkers and most of the gardening jobs I've had since were also fuelled by tea. By contrast, coffee seemed to keep these intelligent office folk afloat; it was the fuel that kept them on point. It was probably only instant coffee back then, but it was a key part of daily life on the tenth floor. How do I know this? I know this because I rescued many plants from compost saturated with coffee dregs. Perhaps they thought they were watering them, but unfortunately it had the opposite effect to giving the plants what they needed. Death by coffee isn't the best way for a plant to go. On occasion, you would find a kindred spirit who was keen to take on any plants that were past their best and save them from the skip (we had no access to a compost bin). Seeing the houseplant that you have been sharing your workspace with for months or even years head down the lift and into the back of a van was just too sad to see. If a houseplant had been given a name, this was a sure-fire indication that it had become part of the team. Don't ask me why, but most houseplants tended to be given male names.

Working in shopping centres was another insight into a world I hadn't ever considered. There, our store cupboard was often close to the security guard's office. This team of uniformed individuals would spend the day watching multiple screens that covered every corner of the centre. If you have ever considered doing a bit of light-fingered lifting in a shopping centre I strongly advise you against it. The security guards have eyes and ears everywhere and are ready to do a pincer movement at any given moment. It was in the security office that we would often see people sit on the edge of the houseplant displays and crush the tradescantias. This wasn't a crime that could be reprimanded – we would simply have to sweep in and resurrect the injured plant or replace it with another specimen that was depressingly likely to experience the same fate. On some days we would arrive to be met by a display that had been completely vandalised. Plants pulled out of the soil and left for dead, litter left lounging amongst the spider plants. This damage would've been done whilst the shops were open and in full view of the general public – simply astonishing.

Map reading and van driving were also essential skills we had to master. Having not long passed my test, driving to an installation in the centre of a busy town was a challenge and my most essential companion was an A-Z of the town in question. The Rascal van was my vehicle of choice as it would turn on a sixpence but unfortunately in winter it would also spin like Torvill and Dean on the ice. Another skill that I hadn't considered I would need was climbing. So much of our work was done at a height. If scindapsus had been planted to trail from the top of an atrium, someone would have to tend to them. Scaffold and harnesses were often essential. Artificial plants were sometime used in places where watering would be impossible, which might sound like a good solution. However, if you're a restaurant owner and are considering such a decoration, please don't. In one garden centre café, the whole ceiling was covered in trellis with artificial ivy wound around it.

Cleaning this for days on end, whilst the café was open, was more than a human neck can take. I suddenly did have something in common with the artist Michelangelo, after all – goodness only knows how he managed to paint the ceiling in the Sistine Chapel in the Vatican without suffering serious long-term injury.

Watering is one of the most important tasks for any gardener to perfect and my time in interior landscaping is definitely where I learnt the art. Watering and placement are the two most likely issues to cause death if done incorrectly. Overwatering houseplants can be catastrophic, as can placing them by a door that opens and closes and lets in outside air that causes a draft. My houseplant placement advice when it comes to drafts is as follows: if you could comfortably stand wrapped only in a towel after a shower without either feeling chilly or burning your bottom on the radiator then a houseplant should find this spot acceptable! Overwatering of plants in public spaces is rarely a problem, however (unless it's death by coffee dregs). It's drought that might kill them off. I discovered there were plants that I wouldn't bother to grow. With our rounds being only fortnightly, the selected plants needed to be tough. Diffenbachias, peace lilies and aglaonema would make it through most boot camps.

This job taught me a great deal. I learned that people often only appreciate plants once they have gone, that smoking is disgusting and that houseplants are often tougher than we give them credit for. But by far the biggest eye-opener for me was discovering how people view gardeners. It was shocking to experience what little appreciation was given to us by office workers and the public. Rarely, if ever, were we spoken to or acknowledged as we went about our caring duties. Being an interior landscaper gave me an insight into so many other work environments and confirmed both how important houseplants are and the people who have the skills to look after them. It's a responsible job that takes time to master. Personally, it also confirmed to me that the clay granules I often planted in were no substitute for real clay – it was time for me to shake off the dust and get my hands properly muddy again.

Sea Salt and Shih Tzus

Flicking through the local paper as I sat with my coffee, I spotted something with irresistible vintage charm and practicality. Others would later describe my find as a death trap and a money pit. This discovery, a car that made me throw all sense and reason out of the window of the makeshift Portacabin that served as the college café, was too irresistible to pass up. Oh, how I wish I could fly by the seat of my pants nowadays but as I have aged, I have become cautious and would probably quickly close the paper and live with the regret – but not back then. I'm hoping that when I reach a ripe old age, I will have renewed bravery and my laissez-faire attitude will reappear with gusto, along with huge costume jewellery and ridiculous outfits. Back then, however, coffee break at college was far from a glamorous affair.

Groups of grubby agricultural and horticultural students would pile in to the Portacabin café all at once, bringing with them mud, muck and hangovers. Our conversations usually ranged from who might fancy whom to who had drunk the most bottles of Newcastle

Brown the evening before. Mind you, at least we were all talking – today, I suspect that mobile phones might replace the laughter and chatter of yesteryear. The agricultural students largely wore rugby tops and jeans or boiler suits. I'm pretty sure that this remains the uniform of trainee country folk today but with the added addition of a Schöffel fleece gilet. The students on the equestrian courses, mostly girls, would add some glamour to the scene. Their tight jodhpurs and long black boots were a necessity, I'm sure, but I suspect they knew how stunning they looked in them.

You could pick out the horticultural students a mile off. I'd like to say that we were not followers of fashion but instead creators of it – we were certainly more flamboyant than the rest. Paisley shirts and tie-dye tops were all the rage, accompanied by cargo trousers, Doc Marten boots and rather inventive, unconventional haircuts. (Some might say 'unconventional' is just a tactful way of saying 'frankly awful'.) Let's put it like this – you could spot a horticultural student as easily as a sunflower growing in a row of cabbages.

We were often mocked for our choice of career by other students, but this never phased us. The majority of agricultural students back then were following in the footsteps of their parents, so their career choice already had a seal of approval. Many of them were earmarked as farmers from birth and some I suspect were given no option but to carry on the family business. Choosing horticulture was almost as unexpected as wanting to be an undertaker. Being different was what most of us craved – we had broken away from the uniforms of school and the watchful eyes of our parents and we were excited about the possibilities of a career in horticulture. Selecting this not very well-trodden path made us feel rather ground-breaking, wonderfully unique and somehow free. At the time it was still considered to be a rather off-the-wall career choice, but we didn't care – it made it all the more tempting and tantalising. I had at last found my people and at the same time found myself.

I should probably confess that I was personally responsible for some of my fellow students' interesting style choices in the form of those abominable haircuts. To make ends meet, I'd set up a mini barber shop in my room. Customers would sit on a stool in the shower, and I would attempt to give them a new look if they crossed my palm with a few silver coins! This side-hustle went very well for a time, until the unfortunate day I made a friend look like Friar Tuck. Word got around that Tammy's Trims wasn't quite up to scratch, and the gig was up. I learnt very quickly that just because you've been taught to prune shrubs and clip grass, it doesn't mean that those skills are transferable to the human head. Looking back, I am rather impressed with the entrepreneurial spirit of my younger self and even more impressed with those fellow students who were stupid enough to be my customers.

Our drinking vessels in the Portacabin café were polystyrene cups and by the end of breaktime there would be piles of broken ones left on the tables – strange how we felt the necessity to dismantle them in such a way or graffiti them with biro. Not only did we leave a trail of mud but a trail of white polystyrene – appalling behaviour. I would hope that recycled cardboard cups or good old-fashioned mugs are their replacement these days. The coffee was just instant and not a patch on freshly ground espresso, or the lattes or cappuccinos we simply can't live without today. Mind you, it was wet and warm and probably as much as we deserved. Back then, I enjoyed heaping sugar into my tea and coffee, bolstering my pathetic penny-pinching student diet of white bread, cup-a-soup, boil-in-the-bag rice, baked beans and cheap wine. I'm convinced that I really lived off fresh air and love, with an added splash of rosé – never did me any harm!

Anyway, I digress. The ad in the paper that day was for a 1972 Series III Land Rover that had been used at Southampton docks. It was up for sale, and I wanted it. Manufactured in the year of my birth, it had to be fate that I'd spotted the advert. Could this vehicle bring me eternal happiness? Without further thought, let alone stopping to take any sensible adult guidance or even considering my very minimal budget, a friend and I headed to the docks.

When we arrived, there she was, parked by the water, riddled in rust but oozing personality. You have probably gathered by now that I love old things – this may explain why my husband is twelve years my senior! The signwriting on the side of the vehicle was something to do with fish. This was obviously slightly off-putting. Would turning up at college with an ancient vehicle that proudly promoted its fishy past do much for my street cred? Doubtful. Would the years of being battered by the salty winds have damaged the body work? Of course. But reason and sense had left me. I'd floated off on a wave of excitement about the adventures my characterful chariot and I were going to have together. After years of hiding in the background at school and being picked last for PE I was going to drive forward in confidence, stand out and do things my way.

So, there I was with a fist of cash in one pocket (my entire life savings) and a dream in the other. Imagine turning up at my weekend gardening job in a Land Rover. I could keep all my tools in the back and even camp in it if I needed to. I couldn't wait to leap into the driving seat to test drive this beauty.

However, as soon as I opened the heavy door the overwhelming smell of fish nearly knocked me off my feet. I am a fish lover, but this smell was off the scale – like nothing else I had ever experienced. This vehicle had obviously been a companion to the fishmonger who had taken his place in the passenger seat. It felt rude to react to the smell, so I did my best to pretend that I hadn't noticed it.

Once my bottom was on the battered seat I was faced with an enormous steering wheel and pedals that were high off the ground. This was to be a completely new driving experience, so different from the mini learner vehicles I was used to. My first concern was to find reverse so that the fishmonger and I didn't meet a watery end in the dock ahead of us. The sound of crunching gears and the roar of the engine accompanied my conversation with the seller.

Not brave enough to test drive my new friend on actual roads I drove up and down the dock, serenaded by the chinking of boat chains and the chanting of seagulls. Once I'd sat in that driving seat, I knew I didn't have the guts to pull out of this deal. Too polite to comment on the stench of fish (perhaps the fishy smell simply belonged to the owner and not the vehicle?) and too concerned about being accused of being a time-waster, I handed over my cash. With the deal done, I drove away from the docks, and suddenly my youthful confidence faded.

I have no doubt that the fishmonger was completely over the moon to shift this mackerel motor; in hindsight he should've paid me to take it off his hands. He was probably jumping into the sea like an excited leaping salmon as I disappeared off into the distance. The fishy smell hadn't been him after all – although the deal he made with me was decidedly rotten – every nook and cranny of my new automobile was oozing with the aroma of the docks and, upon arrival back at college, so too would I.

As I drove with the windows fully down so as not to be intoxicated by the smell of fish, I was seized by panic. What the hell had I done? I hadn't the faintest idea of how to drive my new vehicle properly – what on earth is double declutch? I also hadn't considered the running costs of my new mobile garden shed. As I watched the fuel gauge literally falling by the second, I wondered if I would ever see my parents again. The realisation suddenly hit me that filling this chariot with enough fuel to reach Herefordshire was never going to be affordable. My two Saturday gardening jobs paid me a few pounds a week. Of that, I spent a couple of them on my weekly college disco ticket – was I prepared to miss a night of 'voguing' in my hot pants and the chance to slow dance with someone gorgeous for a few litres of fuel? Tricky decision. But surely now I had the right wheels I'd pick up more gardening work and all would be well – right?

At this time I had recently moved out of the college halls of residence and was living in a small prefab bungalow on a country estate very close to campus. The property was freezing cold and damp (I think it was a kit made from cardboard), but it was the perfect place for my friend and I to experience freedom and play at home-making. We used to enjoy a very organised breakfast at the tiny Formica kitchen table every morning and would spruce up the sitting room with vases of flowers picked from the hedgerows and place magazines at a jaunty angle on the coffee table. It wasn't a place of wild parties as we liked it too much to upset the nearby landlady, but it was a place to drink tea and curl up in front of the fire. After a year of non-stop socialising whilst living in college halls the bungalow was a welcome moment of calm. For some reason, the front door of a Mini lived in the hall. We didn't own it and we didn't ask for it to be removed the entire time we were there. Maybe it was part of a vehicle that another crazy student had invested in.

On occasion, my friend and I would help serve canapés at posh events in the main house, which was adjacent to our bungalow. Most of the time we could be found under the stairs snaffling the devils on horseback. These are prunes wrapped with a rasher of bacon and then cooked. I can't stand prunes but when you're a hungry student you'll pretty much eat anything, particularly if covered in bacon.

Our landlady was just wonderful and the person I wanted to be when I eventually grew up. She would cut her lawn with a ride-on mower at serious speed, whilst wearing an array of incredible diamond and emerald rings. Imagine gardening in precious gems! I once asked her if she feared losing them in the compost heap. It wasn't something that she had considered. From then on, I always kept tally of the number of rings on her fingers. If they'd reduced in number, which they never did, you might have found me volunteering to turn her compost heap. She was simply fabulous and awfully capable. You'd hear her shouting at her two Shih Tzus before you'd hear the engine of the mower and see the green spray of grass clippings shoot up behind her. If you've never had the pleasure of being acquainted with a Shih Tzu then here is my description: energetic toy dogs with either flowing or scruffy long coats. They have wonderful large eyes and most that I have met have been blessed with a strong personality. Read into that what you will!

These two little energetic fluffballs seemed to spend their entire life humping each other right outside our kitchen window. I've never met two more sexually active dogs in my entire life, and I must be honest that however cute they were they completely put me off that breed. If all that raunchy activity was too much for me back then, goodness knows how I'd cope with it now – surely students are meant to be unphased by all things erotic?

Fortunately for me and my newest fishy acquisition, the bungalow was at the top of a steep gravel drive. Without it I'd never have got to college. The Land Rover, which I had affectionally and very appropriately named Delilah ('Why, why, why did I buy you?'), regularly wouldn't start but releasing the brake on the slope and then turning the key seemed to do the trick. However stressful this daily event was, I couldn't help but feel happy sitting in the driving seat looking over the bonnet. Now that the fishmonger's logo had been removed, I felt like a proper horticultural student. On arrival at college – thankfully only about a mile from home – I would never experience actually turning the engine off. Stalling just as I reached my parking space was the norm. It wasn't until I had a proper car that I realised how poor the brakes were, but thankfully I never went very far or fast.

Delilah wasn't with me for long. She required so much welding in her under-parts that her weight continued to increase and she drank fuel like a fish. The father of my boyfriend at the time spent hours trying to rescue this damsel in distress (the vehicle, not me) – thanks to him I think I actually turned a small profit when I sold Delilah to her next owner. I often wonder if she is still on the road today and whether she is still wearing her pungent fishy perfume.

A Rubbish Experience?

Wwhat better place to be than by the sea? Although college was one of my happiest chapters this was to be an even happier one. I'd moved to Dorset to live with Auntie Margie and was working in the parks department in Bournemouth. The chance to reside at Spur Hill Avenue was not to be missed. Her regular dregs parties and wonderfully romantic conversations about the past made up for the damp mattress and the drafts under the doors. What I didn't know when I moved to start this new chapter was that working in all weathers under the watchful eye of the public would be such a positive experience.

I came to realise that gardening in a public park is an honour, and the magic of it is that you can revisit as many times as you like for the rest of your life completely free of charge. Nearly thirty years later, there are still trees that I visit when I'm in the area. There is one tree that I will always be connected to. I was tasked with removing a rather thick branch with a hand saw. It was a challenge, and I can still see the mark on the trunk where the offending branch was finally removed. Being watched by people who are lounging on the lawns as you sweat and struggle is an experience – there's nothing like being put under pressure! When you are working in such a popular holiday destination, it feels as if everyone is on a luxury break apart from you. There's also a row of pine trees on the cliff top that I make a pilgrimage to. I clearly recall planting what I can only describe as pathetic one-foot-tall saplings. At the time I was absolutely convinced that they wouldn't make it past a month, but now they are as tall as church spires. If standing under a tree you have planted doesn't make you feel old, then I'm not sure what will. Planting those trees must be one of my greatest achievements but I had no idea of that at the time. When we drive past them, I always point them out to my son. He seems completely disinterested in my enduring love for them, but I suspect that when I'm dead and gone those trees might start to mean something to him.

On my first day on the parks I was to report to the tin shed that nestled in the rhododendron bushes by the Royal Bath Hotel. (Much to my dismay this shed is no more – it's now been replaced by a car park.) This was my first proper grown-up job, and I was terrified. I was wearing a pair of grey cargo trousers and a very heavy pair of oversized black steel-toe-capped boots. One friend said I looked like a golf club thanks to my skinny legs and giant feet. One thing is for sure, if I'd fallen in water I'd have drowned. Opening that shed door was like stepping into another world. Inside there were men – and only men! I was quite possibly the first woman to work there, and I'm not entirely sure if I was a welcome sight. In time, these men were to become my best mentors and friends. I learnt more from them about how to garden than from anyone else I've met since. On that first day, though, it was intimidating. It was time to buckle down and prove that the college girl had what it took to work on the parks.

As a young girl I used to walk through the green spaces in Bournemouth when on holiday with my parents and marvel at the bedding schemes and the coloured jars that were candlelit in the evenings. To me, a walk through these parks was like a trip to Disney World – it was a magical place. Now it was my chance to tend these beds and refresh the spent candles in the jars. So you can imagine my surprise when, on my first morning, I was handed a litter pick and black bin bags and told to go on the hunt for litter. Hunt for litter! There was no hunting involved – it was everywhere. Before any gardening was done, every member of the parks team would spend a good couple of hours each morning clearing up other people's mess. Fag butts, cans, lolly sticks, condoms, needles and nappies were the main culprits, but I suspect today it would be wet wipes, energy drinks and coffee cups. I can't be sure if this task still falls to the gardeners today, but I'd like people to appreciate the work that goes into keeping our parks safe and clean.

There is an element of risk when gardening in a public place. Needles are the main concern, but broken glass, dog mess and human vomit are also daily hazards. The morning clear up was essential and sometimes quite lucrative. It's surprising how many coins are dropped, and you can soon end up with a satisfying jingle in your pocket. Alas, on one occasion I recall cutting up a £50 note with the cylinder mower – if only my reactions were a little quicker on that day!

We each had our own area to litter pick and mine was a part of the Lower Gardens and Westover Road. It's astonishing how many people would drop their bus tickets right in front of me as if I was their personal butler. Of course, I couldn't react to it then, but I dare you to drop a piece of litter in front of me now as you'll see another side of my personality. It's an unforgivable crime. Washing down vomit and emptying bins all became part of my daily chores but, surprisingly, not for a moment did I dislike this. The satisfaction of looking back to see a clear park and pavement was worth it. This visual sense of achievement is what I value so much about gardening. Being able to see where you have been and the impact you have made is important to me.

Early morning shifts on the park bin round were another eye opener. Get there too early to empty and you'd upset the homeless population, who relied on the contents of the bins for food. We got to know the park residents and would agree on a time, so that everyone was happy. Being in a town before it wakes up is an insight. I was often dropped off down the chines with a witch's broom and a very heavy, cantankerous diesel leaf blower. 'See you at lunchtime,' were the last words I'd hear from my colleagues as they drove off into the distance in the Transit van. There was no way of getting hold of them once they'd gone. Mobile phones were far from commonplace in those days and if you had one, you'd probably have needed a wheelbarrow to move it around! I can't tell you how much I struggled to start that bloody blower. Pulling the rip cord over and over again whilst being watched by dog walkers and families as they headed to the beach was embarrassing, to say the least. There was no way I could fail, so I learned to be determined and discovered how to cope with a flooded engine. I also understood why steel toe-capped boots are important – to kick power tools! On some days when the blower just wouldn't start, instead of admitting to my failings I would go hell for leather with the witch's broom. Looking back now, I suspect I fooled no one as the engine was cold to the touch when my colleagues loaded it up into the Transit.

On one occasion, I was left to work on the roundabout just outside the Royal Bath Hotel. Those of you who know it will appreciate that it's a busy pinch point in Bournemouth. My task was to mow the grass and deadhead the geraniums. Determined to beat the deadline, I raced through the faded geraniums with secateurs. Disaster – I cut the top of my finger and blood spurted everywhere. I was in full public view with cars coming at me from all angles. To stem the flow of blood, I popped my finger in my mouth. That merely led to an even more dramatic scene of a girl with blood coming out of her mouth. A lovely lady spotted my plight and whisked me off to hospital in her rather smart soft top car, which I suspect I might have bled over. When the foreman came to collect me for lunch he would've been met by a barrow of tools and a mower abandoned on the roundabout. As this was my first week at the parks, I can only imagine that he thought I'd jacked it all in and gone to sit on the beach with an ice cream. My finger was stitched and bound up and I was soon back in the tin shed reporting for duty again. I'd learned that panic gardening is rarely successful but it's very hard to know as a new gardener how long a task should take. I'd also learned that deadheading at speed with secateurs was not the right method – fingers were really all you needed.

Working on the parks was when I learned how to keep the gardening momentum going all day. Unless you were a smoker, you couldn't take any additional paid breaks - at one point I almost considered taking up smoking so I too could lean against the side of the van for five minutes! As a result of my daily gardening, I was fit as a fiddle and turfing, digging, planting and mowing all became second nature to me. I truly learned all the major skills of how to garden on this job. Along with practical tasks, the team taught me how to laugh. Not a day went past without something entertaining coming our way. Although this job was low paid and involved plenty of physical work the team were happier than anywhere else I've ever worked.

Lunch breaks at the shed were memorable. On sunny days we would sit in the deck chairs that had been rejected from the beach to eat our sandwiches. A good lunch was vital, even if it was presented in a stinky lunch box. (Is it just me or do lunch boxes always end up stinking however well you wash them?) To garden physically all day plenty of food is essential. I've shared this advice with many horticultural students in the past and many have subsequently contacted me to say how valuable it was. You can't just pop to the shops to grab a doughnut when you're employed to garden. Take more food than you think you'll need, and I guarantee you'll eat it. Hot tea is another essential ingredient to a gardener's day but on one occasion I almost killed off the entire team by making a toxic brew! I thought I would be helpful and had decided to clean the giant teapot in the shed with bleach – thankfully I managed to intercept the mugs just in time. As usual, the men took my attempt to poison them in the right spirit.

In recent times, I have revisited the parks to enjoy the Christmas lights. It still feels so familiar to me; the bond I created with this space remains strong although so much more is expected of it than was the case twenty years ago, when I helped to tend it. Everything is far more razzle dazzle than ever before. On my most recent visit it felt like a glitter ball had exploded; there were enormous twinkling Christmas trees, a giant sparkling deer and gigantic baubles that you could walk through, which doubled as a selfie booth. Coloured jars with candles are no longer enough – the bling has landed! It was so well lit up that I expect you could see it from the moon. The majority of the grass lawn was covered with an ice rink, with people wobbling and hanging onto each other in a desperate attempt to avoid spending the festive season on crutches. When I spotted the ice rink I instinctively said to my son, 'Gosh! How on earth with the grass underneath recover?' When did I become such a party pooper? I'm probably the only person to have given the turf a second thought. My new year's resolution is to be less concerned for the welfare of turf, although I strongly suspect that I won't stick to it. I love every living part of that place where I learned to garden – it was very far from a rubbish experience.

Who's Been Eating My Porridge?

I'm not a morning person, so when I took a secondment to work on the greenkeeping team at the parks department, I knew it was going to be a challenge. The day started at 5.30am and with a love of nightclubbing my hours of sleep were seriously impacted. My ears were often still ringing in the morning from the loud music of the evening before. Each day spent as a greenkeeper started with a cycle to work along the beach front at an ungodly hour. This was truly magical and a great way to wake up. Watching the sun rise over the sea is something everyone should experience, especially when you have the beach all to yourself. Cycling was part of my wake-up strategy. A blast of fresh air and some exercise first thing in the morning was the best way to get into gear. Travel in a car with the heater on and you'll have a job to come to enough to set to work with any effectiveness and you'll miss out on saying hello to the milkman on his rounds. Having moved to another department, I'd also lost my free parking space which also had a lot to do with my enthusiasm for cycling!

On arrival, the experienced greenkeepers and their new apprentice (me) would sit in the shed and receive our duties for the day. These sheds (often known as the bait room) come with unwritten rules. You can't just step in and grab a chair. This particular group of men were long established in their roles and there was an unspoken pecking order that I'd have to learn quickly. I wish one of our lecturers at college had taught me the etiquette of the bait shed in our classes. If you ever find yourself in similar shoes don't, for goodness sake, pick a seat or grab a mug without checking if it belongs to someone. Sitting in someone else's old, grass-stained swivel office chair or drinking from a chipped, tea-stained mug that isn't yours is as sinful as Goldilocks eating the bears' porridge. These claimed spaces are just as fixed as they are in an open planned office and personal space and possession must be respected (the same rules apply when it came to mowers and hand tools – you have been warned!). The truth is that back then I'd be the last to arrive in the shed at tea break so just settled for the vacant chair – with a distinct shortage of female staff loos it wasn't uncommon to have to trek into town for a pee in the public toilets before taking my break. Another word of warning – when you arrive at work this early in the morning you must carefully navigate the moods of your colleagues. Few people can cope with a loud and overly enthusiastic greeting at 5.30am. On the other hand, you don't want to look as if you've only had a few hours' sleep and as a result can't be trusted to mow straight lines. (It is for this reason that I was heavily reliant on a top-notch makeup remover so that all traces of eyeliner from my partying antics the night were gone). To be safe, pitch your morning welcome somewhere safely in the middle – be quiet and calm but look ready for action. Try to avoid yawning too much until you are alone.

You have probably gathered by now that I'm a lover of lawns. That feeling of grass between your toes is one of life's greatest pleasures (well it is for me). As a child, I spent many happy hours lounging in long grass plucking the petals from buttercups whilst dreaming of what life might have in store for me. Another happy memory from my childhood was running about the lawn as my grandfather mowed around my sisters and me. He would create little grass islands for us to leap on to. I'm sure he would've far preferred to go up and down without any disturbance from children and create stripes rather than random circles, but I recall him smiling at us, which was a definite skill, as this expression could be displayed even whilst sucking on a pipe. His pipe was a constant in his life. My sisters and I would often be dropped off in town to go and buy him a tin of tobacco from the sweet shop. No one ever questioned us – I suspect the shopkeeper knew only too well who it was for (one of the benefits of living near a very tiny market town). The resulting tobacco tins were all over the place – one was ceremoniously presented to my grandmother every week with her housekeeping money in. I can't imagine what he'd think of the methods of transferring money today – the idea of BACS payments, contactless cards and paying by using your watch would I suspect have seen him increasing his intake of tobacco!

My grandfather's mower was one of the very early Qualcast ride-ons with a roller and cylinder blades. I loved the sound of that engine. He wasn't a gardener but as this task involved transport, he deemed it an acceptable chore for a non-gardener. There is no way he'd have been caught weeding. My grandfather loved anything with an engine, so it must be from him that I get my passion for cars. Most photographs we have of him picture him leaning against his new motor. We still have this Qualcast mower in the back of a garage collecting dust – it holds too many memories to be disposed of. One day, like a scene from *Chitty Chitty Bang Bang*, I hope it will emerge from its slumber with wings and fly again around the lawn. This magical mowing machine is partly why I have such an affection for lawns, but I never imagined I'd be looking after them for work. Having studied mower maintenance at college I just had to hope that my limited knowledge of spark plugs and blade sharpening would come in handy.

In the greenkeeping team, the most regular morning task was to swish the dew off the bowling greens to dry them before mowing. I say 'greens' in plural because, a little like a chicken run, bowling greens need resting. For this reason, they are often built in pairs but share one clubhouse between them. They were usually locked but on one occasion the door was left open, and I wandered inside. The clubhouse walls were decorated with plaques listing the names of top players from the past. Some time later, I was found asleep in a chair by some eager bowlers. Imagine my embarrassment at being found slumbering whilst on duty – it only happened once, as the shock of being woken by a whole team of people dressed in bright white was enough to prevent it happening again. For a moment I thought I was in heaven and being welcomed by God's helpers.

I digress. To remove the dew from grass a specialist greenkeeper's tool is used – it's called a switch and is basically a pole with a long, fairly rigid cord attached to it. There's an art to using a switch and once you get the knack it's a pleasurable way to pass time. I can't walk across a dewy lawn without thinking back to my days on the greens. Another regular task was brushing any worm casts away with a besom broom. However much as gardeners we valued the work of the worms we couldn't leave evidence of their activity on the greens. If their casts are flattened by a mower they are the perfect place for weed seeds to germinate and there's no room for weeds on a bowling green.

Lawn bowls was an activity I knew nothing about before my time on the greenkeeping team, but I was soon to learn that it is a serious sport that creates extreme competitiveness and argument amongst its players. The expectation that the green would be pitch perfect was high – this wasn't just a pastime, this was a way of life. Groups of players, largely in the prime of their retirement, would arrive dressed in white with the attitude that they were going to play come hell or high water. Their bowls were polished and as far as they were concerned it was game on. It was the greenkeeper's task to tell the bowlers if they were able to play that day – if the grass was too wet it was off. I can only compare this to putting a trampoline in the garden and telling your children they can't jump on it. Toys were regularly thrown out of prams.

Caring for a bowling green is no fool's game. There are big decisions to be made about reseeding, resting, scarifying and watering. It is a little like looking after an ancient document that can only be touched if you're wearing white gloves and it has been unrolled by experts. To preserve the condition of this perfect green square of grass, kid gloves are certainly required, along with care and consideration. Greenkeeping is an art form. It requires record keeping, patience and precision. Timing is crucial and every blade of grass must be of the right length. This is where I learnt to become a dab hand with a pair of edging shears and a cylinder mower. A neatly striped green was expected, and the odd wobble would be spotted in a flash. Mowing a green with a hangover was never a good idea but I do have to confess that I attempted it on a few occasions. Ramps are used to carefully push the mowers onto the grass and never in a million years would you fill a fuel tank on the green or walk across it in muddy boots! In contrast to the diesel leaf blowers of the parks, the lawnmowers here worked on the first pull. They were meticulously maintained and treated like vintage sports cars. There was never any cause for me to use my steel toe-capped boots to kick these beauties into action.

For those who have never experienced the game of lawn bowls before, it is played on a green of perfect grass. The sport has a rich history that dates back thousands of years. Don't ask me to explain the rules – all I know is that in those days the bowls were wooden (they are probably made of some hi-tech rubber now), and each bowl has a bias, which means that it travels across the grass in a curve. I can't presume to know any more than that, as the rules are in fact rather complicated, but anything played on turf and out in the fresh air gets my vote. Don't get lawn bowling confused with ten-pin bowling – there are very few similarities and a keen lawn bowler will be offended by the comparison. To play lawn bowls, it is vital that the surface is completely level, and the grass is short. To achieve this the grass is mown about three times a week. The green is square and has sides of about 30-40m in length. Having a perfectly square area of grass in your care gives you the opportunity to perfect the art of creating stripes with your mower. A wobble or kink is not acceptable and turning badly at the end of each row is a sin. The only way of resolving a bad cut it to brush the grass with a heavyweight stiff broom to disguise the wobble. Every time the green was cut it would be mowed in a different direction – sometimes diagonally, sometimes up and down and, if it was an important match, in both directions. The grass needs to be between 4-8mm in length for the bowl to pick up the expected speed. Around the edge of the green is a ditch where bowls will fall if rolled badly. Bowls that end up in the ditch are appropriately referred to as dead bowls. The edges of the ditch are turf and need clipping and any clippings meticulously removed. It's precision work and on occasion you are tempted to replace the edging shears with a pair of nail scissors and some tweezers.

I know this sounds dreadfully morbid, but these greens had a lot of similarities to a graveyard. Death was all around you as you worked, and silence was the theme tune. The environment was very different to that of the park that I had grown used to. There was a sense of ownership displayed by the bowlers which was never present in the park itself, where any activity seemed to be acceptable. I can't imagine what reception a busker would've been given here, or even a child for that matter. At 5.30 in the morning the nearby roads and park were deathly silent apart from the gentle hum of a cylinder mower, and when a match was being played it was the gardening equivalent to working in a library. The edge of each green was home to benches in memory of dear departed players and the rose beds were fertilized regularly with the ashes of those who chose the greens as their final resting place. I'll never forget the day I was weeding the rose beds and mentioned to a colleague how exceptionally healthy the plants looked. He casually told me that their vigour was probably a result of all the ashes of the deceased that had been spread around them over the years. I was unphased about clearing up vomit and excrement in the park, but the ashes of the deceased did make me wince a little and reach for my gardening gloves. In contrast there was plenty of blood running through the veins of the rugby players who frequented the nearby pitch. On occasion I got to sweep out the changing rooms and listen to the rugby chants before a match. Far more my cup of tea.

Community Service

T he three most common questions asked of me by the public when I was working outdoors in the parks team were: Are you a woman? Why are you doing that? Where are the public toilets? It seemed that spotting a female working with a hoe in a flower bed back in the early nineties was as shocking as an art installation by Tracey Emin. Why was it perceived as such a horrendous thought that a young woman would want to garden by the sea? After all, in the summer my undergarments were a bikini and I would run down to the sea, shed my T-shirt, jeans and boots to go for a swim in the ocean and then drip dry before walking home. I knew full well that no one would steal my mucky old gardening gear whilst I bobbed about in the waves. Not a bad way to end a day. For those who now have an image of Ursula Andress emerging from the sea in her iconic beach scene from the Bond film *Dr. No*, I'm afraid to tell you that you are way off the mark. Being asked if I was a woman was far less of a concern to me, though, than the question 'Why are you doing that?'

Did they assume I was on community service? If so, what were they imagining my crime was? I rather wish I'd had the balls to reply that I was a car thief on day release from prison (now that would've made a good chapter in this book).

Nowadays I can't recall how I replied to these regular questions, or even if I replied at all. After a while, I got used to people stopping to say 'Barry, look – there's a woman working over there.' Barry would often reply, 'Don't be daft, Jean.' I can only compare it to being a caged animal at a zoo: comments about your appearance and actions were the topic of onlookers' conversations, as if you couldn't hear them at all. I don't blame the animals for wanting to nip their admirers or their critics through the wire fencing. If I'd taken this action the aforementioned prison sentence would've been a certainty! Thankfully, the world has moved on and no one would give me a second glance now. I most certainly wouldn't be the only woman tending the parks, and I like to think that women like me helped to make the road far less bumpy for others. I suspect the questions I'd be hearing today would be more along the lines of 'How did you get into this job?', 'What variety of geranium is that?' and 'Where can I get a skinny latte with oat milk?', as well as the perennially popular 'Where are the public loos?' I'm hoping that people don't look down their noses at the gardeners (male or female) to the extent that they used to, but perhaps that might be a little bit of wishful thinking.

On the other side of things, I also enjoyed the people watching and speculated about what I saw. It's a strange human dynamic that goes on in a park and one that was fascinating to watch. So many feel entitled to abuse the freedom of the space, are happy to drop litter, fall into the flower beds drunk or even go for a number two in the rhododendron bushes! They all expect the scars they make on the park to be miraculously healed by those they probably look down their noses at. Unlike many open gardens, where it is acceptable for the gardeners to put up signs with requests such as 'Stay off the Grass' or 'No Dogs, Please', in a public park there are no rules apart from the rule of law. Those that care for the space and love it are expected to tolerate the harm it is subjected to, day after day.

I don't want to paint the park as a place of just mishaps and bad behaviour as it deserves much higher acclaim than that. I watched couples walk arm in arm whilst their children ran on ahead with their buckets and spades to the beach, and it was a place where people took a nap on the grass or learnt to roller skate. Its theme tune in my mind would be 'Don't Sit Under the Apple Tree with Anyone Else But Me,' played by the brass band in the central bandstand. Often buskers could be heard playing sweet music in the hope of raising a few pennies and only occasionally would someone feel that they were important enough to pass through with a booming beat box on their shoulder. I would describe the space as a very large communal garden where so many different lifestyles mingled and where so many memories were and still are made. Where else on the planet can you find people snogging, having picnics, playing ball games, exercising, dancing, dog walking, bird watching, sunbathing, admiring plants… I could go on. It's a joy.

As most park visitors enjoy the space in the summer, they probably assume that in the winter the park gardeners are tucked up in a heated greenhouse with a radio and flask of tea. Far from it. A coastal garden is an exciting space in the summer months and we would garden in shorts and enjoy being under a blue sky, with the main problem being trying to pick a moment to mow when the grass was free of sunbathers. In the winter it's a very different story. Thermal clothing is a must, as is the art of wielding a paint brush. Gardeners need to be a dab hand with a pot of paint as, whatever type of garden you are working in, painting benches, gates and sheds is a regular winter task. In a park, cold winter days are when no one is using the benches so it's the time to act. Although every paint tin will tell you not to apply the contents on a frosty day, I recall many times when I've brushed off the frost from benches with my gloved hands and set to work applying a coat of paint. In the cold, paint takes forever to dry so I got rather good at applying the warning tape over the bench on completion. As I walked away with paint pot in hand, the bench would look like a murder scene cordoned off to keep the evidence intact.

Graffiti isn't something I approve of, but despite that I can't deny that trying to make out what was etched into the wood of the benches was a favourite painting pastime of mine. The messages were a hot bed of love and hate – they weren't beautifully crafted sonnets with dramatic feeling but more often than not along the lines of – 'I heart Joe' and 'I hate Craig'. Of course, 'I Woz Ere' was an ever-popular phrase. Along with the graffiti, the memorial plaques would always catch my attention. Benches were often dedicated to the memory of someone who had now passed away but had spent many happy hours in the park. A lovely gesture and a very good reason to paint them with care. Another task that fell to the gardening teams in both winter and summer was to safety check benches but also the children's play parks. Imagine my delight when I was asked to check out the swings and slides along the beach front. Don't tell anyone but I didn't just check them – I used them enthusiastically!

The assignment that was met with the most praise from the public was when we planted out the bedding. Think of a seaside park, and I'm sure the colourful bedding displays come to mind. The client officer (posh name for the bloke from the town hall) would present us with the planting plans. Our task was to dig over and rake the beds before following their plan to the letter. This preparation work is why I love to dig. I appreciate that in today's modern gardening world no-dig is the done thing but sculpting freshly turned soil with a rake is so satisfying. The pressure was on with this work as once the plants were delivered to the park they had to go into the ground before the end of our gardening day. Leaving them to be stolen off a trailer overnight wasn't an option. We would space the plants evenly using the handle of a trowel as a guide and the aim was to create a completely perfect result using every plant provided. These Victorian-style bedding displays were important as they were judged as part of the Britain in Bloom competition. To win would be a feather in the cap of the town and help to bring the tourists in. Unless this is actually a memory from a strange dream, I recall being selected to lurk in the bushes on judging day with a shovel. My job was to be ready to scoop up any horse manure. One: why the hell were horses involved? Two: why me? I have a feeling that the judges were shown around the town in a horse and cart. When I think back it feels like a lifetime ago that I was pushing a barrow through the parks and a horse and cart doesn't seem that impossible – after all, it was still a time when tea dances were held around the town. For some reason I once ended up on the side lines of a tea dance when inspecting my pavement. So formal, so polite, so wonderful but now that venue is a pub/nightclub where people queue up to enter wearing outfits that would make my now-deceased tea dancers shudder.

Although I'd love to step back in time to the park in the 1990s, I'm just so grateful that it is still a busy thriving space. If these parks were ever lost it would be a crime – I don't think I could get over that. I still need this place; it calls me back year after year and I feel compelled to go and check that it's okay.

Fast Cars and Tyre Pressure

I magine my joy at finding a flat to rent with a shared garden that I could actually afford. Without hesitation, I leapt at the opportunity to move into this rather outdated but spacious ground floor flat. It was furnished (badly) so I was spared the expense and time of finding furniture. This suited me as I could then spend more time concentrating on the garden. It was the first time I had had my own space – albeit a garden that was to be shared with as yet unknown neighbours. As I unpacked the boxes of pots, pans and plates in the kitchen on my first day, I looked out of the window to the unloved plot and pictured neighbourly get-togethers, with rows of runner beans and sweet peas decorating the walls. Renting, and running on a low budget, it was to be a garden largely created by sowing annuals from seed. I was delighted by the fact that the neighbours hadn't shown any outward signs of interest in gardening and so I planned to visit them quick smart to see if they had any objections to me transforming the space.

It was a tricky site, with very high workshop-style buildings on all sides, so light was going to be an issue and finding the right plants a welcome challenge. There were no windows overlooking the garden apart from those belonging to the neighbours and myself, so the privacy was unusually great for a town garden. However, I was soon to discover that the lack of light, heating and a parking space were to be the least of my worries.

As I stood at the window, my plotting and planning for the garden was soon stopped in its tracks. Into the garden wandered a very confident couple. And, horrors - they were both completely naked! I'm guessing that they were only in their late twenties or thirties. He was very skinny, and she was on the larger side – neither of them was *Baywatch* material. The shock was so great that I hid my face behind a just unpacked tea towel. Fortunately, I wasn't holding one of the glass Pyrex dishes my mother had given me at the time as I would surely have dropped it in surprise. I'm not sure if they had seen me through the window but I suspect they had heard me moving in and wanted to make it very obvious that they were staking their claim on the communal space. If I recall, it wasn't really the weather to be comfortably wandering around with nothing on.

'Please tell me I've not got nudists as neighbours. Surely this can't be happening to me?' I said to myself under my breath.

After a few days of residing in my new abode it was obvious that I was definitely sharing this space with nudist neighbours. Whatever the weather they were out. It was a brilliant scheme of theirs to ensure that the garden was only used by them. As a result, I never planted a single seed or turned any soil, but I did manage to build up the courage to hang some washing out on rare occasions.

I managed to stake my claim on the postage-sized garden at the front of the property instead, where there was little danger of crossing paths with them.

My second attempt at creating my own patch of paradise was much more of a success. With my boyfriend at the time, we bought an end of terrace house with a reasonably sized garden. Inside, the stairs were the steepest I'd ever climbed and the rooms small but quaint. It was the perfect place to play house and to begin a life together. Our home was down a very narrow road with limited parking, so we had the usual British fun of neighbours putting out cones to save their space. None of this bothered me – it was a place I pictured staying in for many years. It was my home and I loved it – warts, parking cones, deathly dangerous stairs and all.

Our neighbours on one side were just perfect. They were definitely the type of people that you could borrow a cup of sugar from or ask them to water your plants. On the other side they were far from ideal – it was a busy tyre depot. When you're starting out in life you can't be put off by more industrial neighbours, and after all, I told myself, the constant noise from the air pressure machine was far easier to cope with than nudists. It also explained why the property was within our financial reach. At least I always had someone on hand to pump up the tyre on my wheelbarrow.

We quickly planted the front garden with a crowd of delphiniums and I recall them looking spectacular against the yellow and blue Goodyear Tyres sign. The back garden was a rather naive mixture of tropical plants and cottage garden favourites. If we liked a plant, we'd pop it in with no planning or concern for creating perfect plant combinations. We were both gardeners by trade, learning our craft and loving experimenting with DIY, design and general gardening. Many happy hours were spent painting the breeze block wall white that adjoined the tyre depot and planting up large metal dustbins we had acquired from somewhere with giant cannas. Weekend after weekend we could be found browsing the aisles of Homebase. In typical first home style, every room was painted a different colour – we had green, yellow and even a pink room.

To add to the romance of the story we had rescued two baby doves, and kept them in our garden shed, feeding them religiously until they were large enough to fend for themselves. We decided that we should build a dovecote and keep them. This was a disaster – they were so tame after all our handling that, after one day of freedom, we came home to a frenzy of white feathers on the lawn. The local cats had put paid to the dream of having doves flying overhead. Our garden seemed to be a favourite place for the local felines, and I suspect they thought the doves were a gift to them!

Although it was the most unglamorous of gardens I loved it and I really felt that it was my special place with no one judging its look or design. Our visitors were largely friends in their early twenties, like us, so it was rare for anyone to say anything other than 'nice garden' as the pulled the ring from their beer can. There was absolutely no pressure to create a space with any level of expertise or sophistication. If you pitch yourself as a professional gardener, the pressure to have a perfect plot at home is high by the time you reach a more mature age. I imagine this feeling of expectation must be just as high for interior designers and chefs, and the truth is that by the time you reach your own home you're too exhausted to give your space or evening meal the care and attention it deserves. I am now constantly apologising for my garden but back then I wouldn't have dreamt of doing that.

However, this home-making life that I loved was soon punctured and there was no fixing this tyre. On discovering our relationship was over and the house was to be sold, in dramatic style I decided to spend a night in the hammock in the garden. I can confirm that a hammock is not as comfy as they make out on those holiday adverts when you see some gorgeous person lounging in one. This sleepover was my way of saying goodbye to the garden. Our little experimental plot had given me confidence, given me purpose and given me a window into the life I wanted. My father, as he always did, came to the rescue. He packed all my belongings into an old horse trailer and I waved them off knowing that I wouldn't be requiring a spade for a while. This was to be the first time in years that I had no access to soil, as at the time I was working in a magazine office. It's quite incredible how many tools and handy bits and bobs one can collect in a short space of time. I'd acquired so many that I suspect that when my father arrived home where to store them became reason for a few expletives. My parents had assumed I was sorted but suddenly most of my belongings were heading back their way.

When I shut the door of my little house for the very last time, I was young, free, single and desperately sad. So, what does a girl do with a broken heart and no garden to heal it in? Well, she spends every last penny she has on a soft top, bright red sports car, a fabulous headscarf and pair of dark glasses. If you're going to drive away from what you love you might as well do it in style. Nothing beats driving a coast road with The Carpenters blaring out of your sound system. In the words of Karen Carpenter 'What lies in the future is a mystery to us all. No one can predict the wheel of fortune as it falls.' I had said goodbye to love and was driving into the unknown.

I decided to join a gym to replace my usual gardening keep fit workout and went to the induction session – and then never returned. The thought of bouncing up and down next to those muscle men and women in perfectly matching outfits was too overwhelming. Gardening doesn't require you to be dressed in Lycra or invest in shoelaces that match your headband. The gym was far too intense and far too body beautiful for me. I'm also never that sure if I want to drip with sweat in public (not a good look!). Gardening allows you to keep fit and see the results – if the energy used in a gym was put into turning compost heaps or preparing veg beds the world, as far as I'm concerned, would be a better place. Mind you, I suspect that there is a much higher chance of meeting a new partner at a gym than down the allotments! My compromise was to join the adult tap-dancing class in the church hall. I was beyond appalling and definitely the weakest link in the group, but every single girl has to throw herself into a new hobby where she might meet other singletons – it's the unofficial law. In today's world I'd have joined a community gardening group, where I could've avoided all the embarrassment of attempting step ball changes and back flaps. I never imagined that I would end up on a stage dressed in a homemade, bright red soldier's outfit, attempting to tap dance whilst under the influence of a large amount of wine to calm my nerves. This wasn't where I was supposed to be!

Weekends were spent shopping. Some turn to binge eating or booze to mend a broken heart but I turned to shoes – without a garden I successfully wasted hundreds of pounds in the hope that each pair of shoes would transform me into a different person. I suspect I'd watched *The Wizard of Oz* too many times as a child and was hoping to find the ruby slippers for sale in the high street.

A very memorable pair of shoes (which I now realise were simply ghastly) were stolen from me in a nightclub by the drag act. They were probably about four inches high, open-toed with lots of straps and buckles and they were completely gold. The drag artist had spotted them on me from the stage and asked to try them on after the show. Before I knew it, both she and shoes had disappeared – maybe I had found the magic slippers after all, but someone else was going to benefit from them. I won't ever forget walking back to my digs barefoot in the middle of the night – I had successfully morphed into Bridget Jones and I still blame this squarely on the fact that I'd not only lost my shoes but my garden!

The Smell of Success

For weeks I'd been eyeing up a jumper in a shop window. It was dark green and as soft as a kitten. Today I was going to dash out in my lunch break and make it mine. When I'd been employed in a practical horticultural role in a town, it was never the done thing to do a little shopping in your lunch break. Breaks were shorter, if you got a proper lunch break at all, and you were so hungry that you'd certainly rather spend the time eating than shopping to build up energy for the afternoon. Browsing high street stores in steel toe-capped boots never appealed to me much either. I suspect I'd have been greeted by the shop assistants in the same way that Julia Roberts was in the film *Pretty Woman*. The shopping districts of Bournemouth and Poole might not have been Rodeo Drive, but I think heads would still have turned if I entered Dorothy Perkins in my grass-stained jeans. Now I was working in an office job, however, I could spend a good hour looking for things to buy that I really didn't need. I was soon to discover that wearing gardening scruffs was, in fact, a great way of saving your pennies as these regular walks down town 'to get a little exercise' were becoming pretty expensive. Much to my amazement when I first started a job at a gardening magazine, we were allowed to eat at our desks, so after nibbling all morning I didn't have to waste time on filling my stomach at lunch. This is something I never quite got used to – it seemed so decadent to be able to eat a doughnut or a sandwich and a bag of crisps whilst writing an article. No wonder our keyboards needed professional cleaning. The lady that sat next to me used to regularly eat rollmops at her desk! Her highly perfumed pickled herring fillets certainly made my eyes water and momentarily hindered my proof-reading.

On returning to the office that day with my new purchase I couldn't resist dashing to the ladies to put it on straight away before returning to my desk. As I entered the office, confidently modelling my new garment from M&S, I was met by a wall of silence. I've never before or since stepped into a room of people so quiet – it certainly wasn't the norm at my magazine. No one turned to look at me as I entered; everyone's heads were down. Why hadn't anyone noticed my flashy new jumper? What was going on? It was almost as if someone had died.

A few minutes later I was called into the publisher's office just down the hall, where all would be revealed. I nervously opened the door and sat on the chair in the middle of the room. This didn't feel good – something was up. Had I made a catastrophic error in my 'Jobs For The Month' column? Maybe I'd made suggested that readers should sow their tomatoes outside in January and it had led to a flood of complaints from subscribers. Or had I put petrol in the diesel company car? (I confess that I have once done this and was saved by the AA!) I wish one of these scenarios had been the case but instead I was to discover that the whole team were being made redundant. The magazine was to be closed and I was to collect my belongings and leave straight away. The rest of the team had obviously been told the bad news whilst I was shopping in town, blissfully unaware of the unfolding drama back at the office.

On hearing this, I experienced shock, a sense of bereavement and very sweaty palms. I might have also shed a tear. I'm sure my reaction wasn't helpful to the poor person giving me the news. No one, however professional, cool and calm they are, likes being faced with a blithering wreck. Although none of us had done anything wrong, it felt as if the jury had sent us down for attempted murder. My world had fallen apart. If you've experienced being made redundant then you'll know that feeling of loss and fear. Would I ever eat again (I'd certainly fit into the jumper easily if that was to be the case)? Would I end up living in the car? Should I steal the loo roll from the toilet before I exited the office for the last time? How could I recover from this? For me, it was the first time I'd experienced the cold, hard reality of business. I had made this publication and the team that created it my life. I loved all the new experiences I'd had: photoshoots, finding cover locations, planting up containers to be featured in the magazine. Although I had never intended to spend most of my days sitting in a swivel chair, I'd landed a job that offered variety and the opportunity to discover so many different aspects of horticulture. It had the eclectic mix that a Gemini must have to survive and thrive in a workplace – boredom and repetitive tasks are not an option for people born under this star sign. It was also the first job I'd had that my non-gardening friends looked upon as being reasonably socially acceptable. As I heard the news that the magazine would be no more, I was convinced that I'd never make it back into a situation like this again. The publishing world is tough, and so tough decisions have to be made in ivory towers if a title isn't profitable. When I became an editor later in life, this early experience of redundancy served me well. The realisation that a publication has to be profitable ensured I was always very familiar with the company's bottom line, and I also made a habit of trying to protect my own finances by avoiding too many walks downtown! (Mind you, I think this lack of a brisk lunchtime walk might have had a detrimental effect on the size of my bottom.)

Working on a magazine had given me stability, a little bit of kudos and a decent wage packet (oh yes, and the excitement of going in to WH Smiths and putting your magazine in front of the likes of *Vogue* and *Country Living*. This naughty act had to be done with very stealth movements). This was my first magazine job and upon joining I had barely used a computer. When my mother told my old English teacher from school that I was now working at a magazine office she just couldn't believe what she was hearing. It's fair to say that I was the last person from my form that she'd expect to take up this type of work. English was not my best subject at school.

I was the office junior with a capital J and I always appreciated how lucky I was to have this chance. Not having any journalism qualifications, I was nurtured by a wonderfully generous editor and had been shown the ropes repeatedly. The internet was just the stuff of science fiction back then, so I spent my days hugging the office dictionary and thesaurus for reassurance. If these two essential books weren't on my desk, panic would set in – I literally couldn't get through an hour, let alone a day, without their company. Identifying plants without the help of the world wide web was also a challenge back then. All you had to go by was your own knowledge, nursery catalogues and reference books. If I had to go back to those days now, I'm sure it would be like working underwater in a blindfold whilst struggling for air. This lack of online information made it vital that at least a few members of the team knew something about plants and this is where I came in. Knowing my fuchsias from my geraniums was the only reason I had a seat in the room. I might have been the lowest common denominator, but I was there by the skin of my buck teeth.

If I recall correctly, it was only the editor who had email at this point and so most of my days were spent on the phone, answering queries and checking that the telephone numbers for suppliers and stockists that were to be published in the magazine were correct. Back in those days, the landline for a company or open garden was essential – and people actually picked up the phone! In today's magazine offices, I doubt you would even hear a phone ring but it was constant back then. We also received handwritten letters from readers – imagine that! If we ran a competition, a flock of postcard entries would fly in through the letter box and be placed in a large sack. The office was full of reference books and had drawers of useful brochures filed in alphabetical order – these files were our internet. Unlike the modern offices of today, we had lots of stuff. I know you'll find this hard to believe, but I was often sent to the local library to do research. The digital revolution that is the internet has made my memories of magazine life in the mid 1990s almost unbelievable to reflect on. We had to come up with our own, totally unique ideas and learn the skills to describe what we envisaged. There was no Pinterest or Instagram to plunder for inspiration.

I'll never forget my first day at this dream job. As I walked the long corridor towards my new desk, I passed the office of a well-established garden writer. She had stacks of paper and empty mugs everywhere and was typing at the speed of light. I was in awe as I watched her fingers dance across the keyboard at speed. To me, she seemed to be a goddess, with gardening information literally flowing from her every pore. She was who I aspired to be, and at that point I had no idea how many light years away I was from achieving my dream.

When I was eventually trusted to write a story, it took me hours and hours and when I submitted what I thought was the final version, it was almost always returned to my desk decorated in red pen. My keyboard skills were non-existent and my sentence structure deplorable. My first feature was to cover the subject of front gardens and I remember spending a sleepless night coming up with headline after headline – none of which made the grade. 'Up Front, Full Frontal' (what type of magazine did I think I was working for?) and 'Front and Centre' were just some of my dismal and quickly rejected ideas. Although working my way from the bottom up was challenging, I'm an ambassador for learning on the job. It was fear that taught me. Being so unsure made me check, check and check again. If you assume you know nothing, you are in a much safer place than if you think you know it all. I learned to ask questions and listen carefully to instructions – if only I had done this at school. Then, just as I'd started to get a feel for the job (two years after starting), my journey was to end abruptly. My lucky ticket had expired. What would I do?

Well, the first thing I did was return the gorgeous green jumper, of course, as my contract didn't allow me any redundancy package.

With tears in my eyes, I handed it back over the counter and told a little white lie that it didn't fit. Thank goodness for the lenient returns policy of good old Marks and Sparks.

So, what next? I felt as if I'd got my Golden Ticket and made it through the gates of Willy Wonka's Chocolate Factory only to be eliminated from the tour. It was time to head back to reality. For me, reality meant returning to the world of interior landscaping once more. This time, I would be maintaining the plants alongside selling plant displays to businesses – not in person but on the phone. Being a telephone sales rep was the last job on earth that I wanted but needs must. Thankfully, my attempts at selling plants were greeted with some enthusiasm – not always, certainly, but sometimes. On the bright side, there were no shops anywhere near the rural portacabin parked up by the company skip. Telephone sales was about as far removed from the exciting world of journalism as you could get. Instead of deadlines to make, I had targets to hit. To top it all off, my manager had read somewhere that placing a mirror on your desk so that you could look at yourself whilst selling was helpful. Helpful? It was bad enough listening to my own voice all day, but to see the words coming out of my mouth was unbearable. Nevertheless, I was grateful for this job. It made me realise that whatever it took I had to make my way back to the heady smell of rollmop herrings and the well-turned pages of my dictionary.

Valentine's Day Drama

Is there anyone out there who truly enjoys the prospect of Valentine's Day? You are either under pressure to give a gift or under pressure to receive one. I'm sure that if you think about it, you'll probably come to the same conclusion as me – it's a lot of stuff and overpriced nonsense! February is a dreary month as it is, without the added annoyance of being bombarded by promotions about love and lust. Even though I'm happily married the whole thing still grates on me, so goodness only knows how awful it is for singletons. For the record, my husband would never dream of buying me flowers as I'm so fussy about where they come from, how they look and how they are presented. He claims he could never get it right so has opted out of this stressful purchase altogether. I admit it – I am a flower snob (but I also suspect it's a great way of him not getting involved in the whole Valentine thing).

My negative feelings towards this day stem back to school (most things in life do). At senior school, some clever clogs came up with the idea that children could buy a carnation for a potential boyfriend or girlfriend, and their gesture of love would be delivered direct to the desk of the object of their affection on the day. Some would receive fistfuls of flowers whilst others like myself would get none – or the odd one from my sympathetic parents. What a wonderful way to start a popularity contest. Genius. The fallout of this is that I'm not a fan of carnations, Valentine's Day or popularity contests of any kind.

The only good thing to come out of this 'romantic' day is that hard-working florists have customers flocking to their stores after a quiet January. Without this annual event they would have to wait until Mother's Day or Easter for a fresh flurry of much needed sales. It's tough being a florist as your wares are short-lived and people expect the highest quality at a moment's notice. The pressure is on to sell when the blooms are at their peak. If you can afford it, I'm all for buying a bunch of flowers for yourself occasionally to support them. A florist is essential for life's important moments such as weddings and funerals so we should all buy flowers more regularly, so that they're still there when we really need them.

One memorable year, living up the road from a busy florist, an opportunity arose (get it?) to help with door-to-door deliveries on Valentine's Day. I thought it would be fun to be part of the madness. My job that day was to wait in the work room for orders to be completed, load them into the van in line with either the promised delivery time or the direction of travel for the order and drive them to the love of someone's life. On this frantic day the workroom was a hot bed of activity and had been since the early hours of the morning. Foliage stripped from stems littered the floor and red ribbon was flying everywhere. There was no tea drinking or chit-chatting: this was a full on, all hands-on-deck kind of day. The logistics of working out which flowers were needed to fulfil the deliveries and also having enough on the shop floor for customers who walked in off the street was enough to blow my mind. Fortunately, my duties as driver didn't stray into this area!

As I waited for the next batch of bunches to be completed, I watched the florists make beautiful creations at speed. What started with one stem suddenly became a garden in their hands. There is an art to this, and part of that art is costing the flowers as you build the bouquet. If money is no object then of course you can create a showstopper, but if your customer only has a budget of £15 then you have to be a magician and make something out of nothing – or really go for it with the ribbon! Every florist needs a calculator constantly working away in their head as well as a lot of creative flair.

This delivery driving adventure occurred well before the days when you could order flowers online. Now we can happily type our personal message into a box on a website and not have the embarrassment of speaking the actual words to a human being. In those days, the florist would write down the message that was relayed over the telephone or by the customer standing in the shop. I found it hilarious hearing the florist repeating the messages – 'So, your message is: To my Cupcake. With love from your Pork Chop?' or 'Can I just check your message, sir? "I promise I am going to leave my wife this time."' I suspect that over time the florists become very familiar with the serial adulterers in the neighbourhood! Customers who were physically in the shop would whisper their chosen words in the hope that only the card-writer would hear them. Think of being at a pharmacist trying to explain that you have a boil in an unfortunate place – it's an equally embarrassing moment. I'm sure that these messages keep the florists topped up with excellent material to share with their families when they go home. With many of the bouquets being sent from 'A Mystery Admirer', the florist – especially in a small town – is the keeper of many secrets.

Bouquet after bouquet was loaded into the van and I was off with my A-Z in hand. That day was an insight into the life of a delivery driver. One-way systems, dead ends, no parking, traffic jams, incorrect addresses and a myriad of other unexpected problems had to be faced. They were far too busy at the shop to receive calls from me seeking extra directions – I'd have to work it out and use my common sense. When I say calls, I'd like to stress that even if I did feel inclined to call, they'd have been made from a public telephone box. Mobile phones weren't an option for me back then.

I was soon to discover that this job wasn't just about driving. There was a lot of running involved. Parking in a dodgy spot where the risk of a penalty notice hangs over your head means a quick delivery is vital. One of my first deliveries was to the top floor of a block of flats. I ran up the concrete stairs at a pace as I was eager to avoid getting to know the traffic warden when I returned to my vehicle. When I got to the top, I knocked on the door to be told to sod off with my flowers! This wasn't the reaction I had expected from my first delivery. In my naivety, I'd imagined that I'd be met with gushing thanks and even maybe a few happy tears. As the door was slammed in my face, I wondered why the bouquet had been met with such disgust. Imagine not wanting a bunch of flowers! Was it a failed apology for an affair or from an unwanted pursuer? Not daring to return to the shop with an undelivered bouquet I left it by the door and legged it back to the van. My theory that Valentine's Day wasn't a joy for everyone was quickly being confirmed. It wasn't just me who had a problem with it.

Walking down a street of terraced houses was just brilliant. Talk about curtain twitching. 'Jean at number 24 has just had a bouquet arrive. I bet that's not from her John!' – these are the sort of calls I imagined would be going on between neighbours as I drove away. I'm sure I didn't imagine that there were a few disappointed looks as I walked past a house and on to the next. Later in the day, I was delighted to be delivering in the posh part of town. I was heading to the land of gated properties, long drives and homes where I suspected chandeliers hung and hot tubs bubbled. This was surely going to be a breeze. The size of the bouquets had tripled with this more sought-after postcode. It seems that money can buy you love – well, that is if you measure your levels of love on the number of roses you are given.

I arrived at the first property to be met by electric gates. I leant out of the van window to announce my presence into the speaker. The gates slowly opened, and I slowly drove through them. As I admired the neatly clipped hedges that flanked the long drive, I was suddenly aware that my presence was not welcome. Two very large, very loud and very angry Dobermans were pounding towards me. Even in the van I felt fearful. I continued to drive slowly towards the house, trying not to run these canine bodyguards over. Imagine heading back to the shop with blood splatter on the van! As I pulled up outside the house, the dogs stood barking by my driver's door. What should I do?

I lowered the window just a little and shouted 'Hello, flower delivery!' No reply. Was the owner otherwise engaged? I imagined them lounging in a bubble bath with a glass of champagne whilst I took my life into my own hands. There was no way I was going to get out of this vehicle and meet my death on Valentine's Day. I didn't want the dreaded date of February 14th on my headstone, thank you very much. Should I attempt to throw the bouquet out of the window towards the front door? What would be the consequences of a bouquet bouncing off the wall? It was a tempting solution, but I didn't fancy having to pay for the damaged roses – this was a serious bunch of blossoming bling. I had visions of the family pets tearing the bouquet into a thousand pieces and the owner opening the door to find a horrifying scene, the opposite of affection.

After about a quarter of an hour, the dogs were still barking and the windows of the van were starting to steam up. These bodyguards weren't going to stand down. I turned the van around and sped up the drive, hotly pursued by my four-legged friends. I can remember to this day watching them in the wing mirrors as they ran behind. Concluding that there was no other option, I dropped the bouquet out of the window just by the electric gates then got the hell out of there. No complaint was ever made so I can only assume that they eventually found their way to a cut-glass crystal vase.

By the end of the day, I had experienced nearly every human emotion. I had witnessed the stress of the florist, the hilarity of the gushing messages, anger from the recipient of an unwanted bunch of flowers, the fear of being trapped in a vehicle by giant dogs and the disappointment of a customer whose bouquet didn't get delivered on time, but also tears of joy and the elation of the recipient of a surprise gift. By the time the last of the bouquets had been delivered, night had fallen and the shop was naked. Every red rose had been sold. This day of hearts and flowers was over. Who knew that delivering flowers would be so eventful?

Did it change my view of this annual event? No, not really. I would prefer that we revert to the Victorian custom of choosing flowers for friends, enemies and lovers. Back then, each bloom was chosen for its hidden meaning and not its beauty. In floriography (the language of flowers) the gift of African violets means vulgar minds, basil – hatred, Michaelmas daisy – after thought, yellow roses signify jealousy and striped carnations mean refusal. Obviously, many of the flowers mean true love and other gushing gorgeousness but I'm drawn to the not-so-romantic meanings – far more mischievous.

Brace Yourself

In my mid-twenties I took the decision to sort out my teeth. I suffered from an undershot jaw and buck teeth and, as a result, was very shy about my appearance and unhappy about being featured in the gardening magazine I was working on. As an office junior it was becoming ever trickier to avoid the camera. I was often performing practical gardening tasks to create step-by-step images for the publication – to avoid showing my teeth you wouldn't get a smile from me. My mother had tried to persuade me to have braces in my teens, but I just couldn't cope with the thought of that at school. When you are a spotty thirteen-year-old with no end of nicknames, being condemned to months of mortifiacation every time you open your mouth doesn't sound like it will do much for your confidence. I just wasn't up to the challenge then.

However, I had now had enough of looking like Bugs Bunny. In I went to the orthodontist and out I came with a full set of railway tracks and a head brace. Not just any railway tracks – golden railway tracks! Whatever was I thinking, you might ask? Well, the orthodontist had assured me they didn't show up as much as silver ones, so would be less noticeable. In hindsight, I'm unconvinced by this theory. In order to complete the arduous task of moving my teeth by well over 1cm I had to wear the head brace for as many hours of the day as I could face. This contraption is not attractive. Thick elastic bands hold it in place over your head, as metal bars on both sides are pushed into a slot in the brace. In my determination to complete the course with speed I would wear the brace all night, when driving *and* at my desk at work. After the initial shock my colleagues soon became accustomed to working with a rather strange-looking desk mate. It was tricky to talk clearly and impossible to eat and drink but, with the end goal in sight, I was prepared to do whatever it took. I'll never forget the looks I got from fellow drivers as they pulled up beside me in their car at the lights. One association comes to mind – Hannibal Lecter. However, there was no chance of me eating anyone. Have you tried to chew in railway tracks?

Part way through my eighteen-month orthodontal ordeal I found myself in the spotlight – not for long but for a moment. A call came into the magazine from Lorraine Kelly's breakfast television show. The producers were looking for someone to stand in for their regular presenter the following morning to do the gardening slot. The subject was garden features. My office colleagues selected me for the task. Quite why I was chosen I've never fully understood, but this is how, filled with a heady mix of fear and enthusiasm, I found myself behind the wheel of a large company car that I was only just about capable of driving, with a boot full of gnomes, cherubs, stone animals and other wonderfully varied garden features. I had begged and borrowed from local garden centres and DIY stores who thankfully were happy to loan me the items for the following morning. After achieving this in such a short time I've always been convinced that I'd smash the treasure hunt challenge on Sir Alan Sugar's *The Apprentice*.

In preparation for this unexpected event, I had turned my entire wardrobe out onto the bed to find an outfit, packed and hit the road at record speed. What do you wear when you are going on TV? I opted for black trousers and a shocking pink cardigan (which in hindsight was hideous). It was the exact outfit I had worn on my first date with the man who is now my husband, so I was convinced it was lucky for me. There had been no time to shop or get my hair done after collecting all the garden ornaments. I was being thrown in front of the camera as I truly was.

Not only was this my first TV experience but it was also my first ever drive into central London. I was out of my depth. I must have driven up and down one-way streets for hours clutching my A-Z of the city. In the end, I had to pay a taxi driver to lead me to the hotel – although the description 'hotel' is a little generous. Mostly, I was just relieved to be at my home for the night. I spent the evening rehearsing how I would answer all the possible questions that might be thrown at me about how to place a gnome or how to give an aged look to a new stone feature. To describe my feelings as nervous would be an understatement. (For reference, in my opinion, gnomes should be placed slightly out of sight so they peer from behind some greenery – never allow them to be in full view. As for aging stone features, the answer to this is to paint on a coat of natural yoghurt or a mix of cow manure and water. Lovely!) The hotel room was the smallest room I have ever tried to sleep in. If I was to remove all the furniture and lie on the floor in a star shape, I could've made physical contact with every wall. It was airless and, to make it worse, bright orange. I certainly felt like I had been Tangoed. It was the worst night's sleep I have ever had in my entire life. I slept better the night I was induced to give birth to my son!

The next day was to begin at silly o'clock when I had to make my way to the studio with all my gardening paraphernalia. I managed to negotiate the London streets with a little more skill on this occasion. Being so early in the morning, the traffic seemed less fraught and as a result, so was I. Upon arrival I was sent to makeup where I was spruced up alongside the late John McCririck, the fabulously eccentric racing pundit. I remember looking at his hands and thinking that I probably had the same amount of gold in my mouth as he was wearing on his fingers. After the makeup artist had finished, I'm pretty sure that I looked as orange as the hotel bedroom. Not being a wearer of foundation, it was a bit of a shock to see my fully made-up face looking back at me from the mirror. And then it was time to be ushered to do my piece on camera.

My segment took place by the side of the Thames, and I was to talk the weather presenter through the selection of garden features I had chosen and explain how to place them in a garden. You'll be eagerly awaiting all the details of how it went - whether I looked at the right camera, if I was in line to be the next big thing, or whether I dropped the gnome - but I'm afraid that I really can't recall it in any detail at all. Maybe my mind blocked it out. I do remember telling the viewer to avoid animal figurines that aren't in scale with each other. It's been one of my bugbears in life – why would you place a figure of a giant squirrel in a garden next to a miniature elephant? This design faux pas happens far more than you would imagine. My other top tip was to refine your choice of features. One or two stunning focal points are far more successful than an eclectic mix. Look at it like this – one romantic partner is enough for most of us, two is potentially exciting but perhaps a little risky and more than that will just make your head spin!

What I do recall distinctly is how abruptly my experience in the spotlight ended. Everyone involved simply moved on to another segment with no 'thanks' or 'well done' – nothing. Was I simply terrible or had I pulled it off? I was none the wiser. Now I am older and more experienced I understand the pressures of a live show. There is no time to deal with nervous stand-in so-called experts. Getting up that early every day to face the nation is not something that I could do so I can forgive them for the lack of feedback. I watched the recording just the once. That was enough! The pink cardigan quickly made its way to the charity shop – it might have been lucky but bright pink really wasn't my colour and seemed to clash terribly with my golden braces.

This one-off opportunity has stayed with me as a clear memory as it was watched by my father as he lay in his hospital bed. Apparently, the nurses wheeled a TV into the ward so he could see his daughter's television debut. It was to be the last time he would see me. I often wonder if he died assuming that I was going to become a leading light of the TV gardening world. In reality, the chances of someone sporting a mouthful of golden braces becoming a regular on the Lorraine Kelly breakfast show were thin but I'm so grateful I had this opportunity as I know that this appearance, however bad, would've delighted my father. Knowing that he would be watching encouraged me to take the chance in the first place. It was a day of so many emotions – it was and still is the thought of what my late father would think of the things I do that spurs me on. I'm convinced it's his spirit that has made me say yes to many things in life. Losing a parent in my early twenties made me realise that life is uncertain, and opportunities must be taken. You seldom regret the things you have done and often regret those that you haven't.

So, did my little dance into the world of gardening on the small screen leave me eager for more? No, not really. I'm not sure I have the looks, the nerves or the wardrobe. I love to see the reaction of an audience and respond to them, and television doesn't really offer that sort of on-the-spot feedback. Unless Graham Norton or Jonathan Ross want to give up their chat-show hot seats to a welly-wearing gardener then I think the world of TV is going to be fine without me.

Dented But Still Going Strong

After being made redundant twice by publishing companies, and working in some less than enjoyable jobs, I decided that it was time to be my own boss. (You'd be excused for thinking that I had something to do with the closure of both the magazines in question, but I can promise you, I'm not guilty.) At this time in my life, I had little in the way of responsibilities and was free to take the giant leap. Saying goodbye to regular monthly pay cheques takes bravery and a little bit of stupidity mixed in for luck. My plan was to open a shop and sell gardening gorgeousness in the way of pots, plants, tools, and gifts. I'm not quite sure where this notion of opening a shop came from but I was set on it. Aside from running a very lucrative grocery store in my grandmother's pantry as a child with my sisters, the only retail experience I had was a little time in a garden centre as a teenager and selling bags of horse manure by the side of the road when I was young, which was pretty lucrative. It seems that people will buy s**t!

To prepare myself for all that this challenge would throw at me, I enrolled on a business course. This was an eye opener – I thought my idea was slightly risky until I heard what other people on the course had in mind. Many of their concepts would've made Sir Alan Sugar's eyes water. We had a wannabe undertaker who had absolutely no previous experience of that industry and a lady who had plans to deliver cooked breakfasts to people's doors but hadn't considered quite how she would single-handedly cook and transport them before it would be more like lunchtime! Standing in front of a group of complete strangers and explaining what you planned to do was a vital part of the process. If they didn't understand your business within a few minutes, you weren't on to a winner. For something to work, the idea can't afford to be the slightest bit cryptic. I suspect that's why my horse manure business as a child was so successful – there was no way of complicating that. You really have to do what you have written on your imaginary tin. Complicated just doesn't cut it. People rarely read signs and leaflets so obvious is the way forward.

At the time, there was no such thing as social media. Printed leaflets, business cards, signage, advertising and making face-to-face contact with other local businesses and actual human beings was your only way of letting people know you were open for business. Breakfast meetings with other local entrepreneurs and walking the streets with leaflets were the ingredients to success. Now, I'm relieved to say, you can avoid all this legwork and market your idea from the comfort of your sofa with the help of your mobile phone. The only advantage to the old school techniques of marketing is that you have to answer people's questions about your idea in person. You can see first-hand if their eyes have glazed over or if they greet the concept with a look of confusion. As deflating as it can be, it's better to see the lack of interest in people's eyes before you open your business. It can save a lot of time. And money!

Our tutor was refreshingly honest and didn't hold back when it came to giving his opinions. His tactic, I'm sure, was to put people off making expensive mistakes and for that he needed commending. In fact, I now recall that at the start of the course he announced that his role was to stop us going into business. He'd probably heard every hairbrained idea before. Eye-rolling was a gesture we got used to from him over the weeks. After a few sessions I presented him with a business plan that seemed to pass muster, so I was off. The fun part was to begin.

Creating your own brand for a physical business is one of the most fantastic experiences you can have. Nearly every part of your new venture is on show – if you're spending valuable money on printing promotional material it must be right the first time. I relished the challenges of finding a property, looking for stock and designing a logo. My creative juices were flowing to such an extent that I almost couldn't keep up with myself. I was setting this business up and doing everything completely alone; from the concept right through to painting the walls and cleaning the windows. Flying solo meant I didn't have to consult anyone or get their permission – I had complete freedom of choice and no one to blame if I made a mistake.

There is no denying that opening a shop of any kind is hard work, but it can also give you an incredible feeling of euphoria. You've bought into the idea to such an extent that failure just doesn't appear to be an option: nothing and no one can put you off the idea. You're like a teenager in love. However, I'm afraid

I'm here to tell you that, as in any relationship, failure is in fact an option.

Having spent a couple of years sourcing gardening paraphernalia for magazine shopping pages I decided I was adequately qualified to choose stock that would tempt the customers. But before I could buy anything, I needed to find premises. An opportunity came up to rent a shop in the very quaint market town of Wimborne in Dorset. The shop was old and oozed character. It fitted perfectly with the traditional image I was eager to present. In hindsight, which, as many will tell you, is a wonderful thing, choosing an idyllic market town was my first mistake. Quaint equals quiet! Mind you, having recently revisited my old retail stomping ground I was thrilled to see how buzzing the town is now. For a moment I was slightly sorry I hadn't stuck at it for longer.

What I should have done back then before signing the lease was spend time sitting outside the shop, making notes of how many people passed it on an average day. The shop I'd fallen for was tucked away down a side street. This made it affordable but reduced the footfall dramatically. If I was to set up shop again, I would heed the advice given by Kirstie Allsop and Phil Spencer – LOCATION, LOCATION, LOCATION.

My market research wasn't up to scratch, partly because I was too excited to get going but I suspect that even if I had done my due diligence, and my research had revealed a low footfall, I'd have talked myself into thinking it would be okay anyway. I'd found my shop and nothing, even the potential lack of customers, was going to hold me back.

Once the keys were in my hands, there was no time to waste as every day the shop was left empty, I was wasting money. The race was on to find a counter, buy and layout the stock and arrange for the phone to be connected. I'd bought a vintage watering can onto which I'd asked a signwriter to paint my logo. This can was proudly hung outside the door well over head height and signalled that I was nearly ready for the grand reveal. Unfortunately, it was up for only a few days before it was pulled down by a group worse for wear after leaving the pub opposite and kicked around the market square. I was absolutely devastated when I found it lying in the street when I went to open the shop the following morning. I still have that can sitting outside my front door. It's dented but still going strong – a motto for my life.

After I had got over the heartache of my watering can, I found I was in retail heaven. Every morning I would park on the outskirts of town (shopkeepers can rarely afford the car parking charges) and walk my faithful Jack Russell along the river to the shop. There were days when it felt as if I was in the opening scene of the movie *Notting Hill*. You know the scene – Hugh Grant walks down the street as all the market stall holders are smiling and chatting, and customers are filling their baskets with seasonal goodies as summer turns to autumn and into winter and then it's spring again and all appears to be well with the world. It was rather wonderful to get to know a town so well and begin to spot familiar faces and regular patterns of activity. Opposite my shop was a dental practice. Although it's very heartless to admit it, I quite enjoyed seeing terrified people go in. I'd hear the drill and wait to see how they looked when they left. (Most were holding their faces in pain!) Just in view, if I stood on the doorstep of the shop, was the Minster. Watching the comings and goings of this religious building was a mixed blessing. Observing wedding guests struggling to walk along the rather uneven flagstone path in their high heels was always entertaining and seeing stunning brides arrive in highly polished cars was just delightful. However, as my fellow shopkeeper Hugh Grant knows only too well, for every four weddings there is a funeral, which is bound to sadden the mood. Other than being a nosey bystander of these life-changing events, days went by in a very uneventful way. Wet days were dreadfully quiet, and Wimbledon Week was monumentally silent – the high street was almost as bereft of customers as it was in the recent pandemic lockdown. I had no idea how popular tennis was until I opened a shop.

What you soon realise is that being a shopkeeper is like being a lone goldfish in a bowl. Everyone can peer at you, tap on the glass and make comment, but you can't respond or escape. You are trapped in a shop and can't escape the daily visits from folk who are so desperate to hear the voice of another human being. You must smile through it all and take hit after hit. I've never been one for answering back, which was probably a very good thing for public relations. Some customers are browsers, others are buyers, and the majority of both types are lonely and want a chat! I had one gentleman who came in almost every single day at the same time, picked up a jar of my gardener's chutney to read the label and would then leave. He never spoke a word and he never bought a jar. Asking people to leave, however boring or strange you find them, is absolutely not an option – unless of course they are shoplifters. Along with the constant requests for charity raffle prizes also comes the almost daily requests for free gardening advice. Once word gets out that you're a soft touch you are finished! People would come in carrying small, clear plastic bags containing a diseased leaf or two. They were going to stand at my counter until I came up with answer to their problems. It made me think how glad I was not to be a pharmacist. Being shown angry spots, mysterious rashes or troublesome verrucas and being expected to provide a miracle cure must get rather testing. I'll take a diseased leaf over athlete's foot any day.

Owning a shop was the end to holidays and days off for me. If you start the habit of putting up a 'Back in Five Minutes' or 'Closed for the Day' sign, it is the beginning of the end. Your customers will assume you aren't interested enough in their custom to bother opening and give up on you. There's also the incredible temptation of closing a little early on quiet days to resist. The last half an hour in the winter when darkness has fallen and your home is calling you is a killer. Unless you can afford an assistant, you will be in that shop day after day. You need to mentally prepare for that and make sure that after you have dusted everything three times and re-done your window display for the tenth time in a week that you have something else to do. In hindsight, I should have taken up knitting. If you do find something else to do, then of course you must be ready to drop the knitting needles mid-stitch as soon as a customer enters. You need to suddenly give the appearance that you are rushed off your feet and the shop is keeping you on your toes. A proprietor that tucks themself in a corner with a book or jigsaw puzzle hardly gives the impression of success. Customers would often ask if I was busy to which I would always reply "Yes, very." I didn't view this reply as a lie but more as a bit of positive marketing.

I learned the value of money doing this job. Getting people to buy things isn't easy. My best sellers were the most unexpected items. Scented lavender water for the iron was a hit – if I could help it the ironing board would stay folded up in the corner, so I've never used such a decadent liquid, but it seems some people are ironing fanatics. Strangely, garden trowels don't sell well at all. My shop was small so I couldn't have the same items on offer all the time. Moving and hiding things was essential – it was vital to put out what appeared to be new stock and create the perception of a high turnover venue. The biggest issue for a small concern is that many companies only want to sell you large quantities of an item. I had little to no chance of selling 100 rosemary-scented candles or ten pairs of size four gardening shoes. I am reminded of this fact often, as I still have a drawer full of gardener's keyrings that I mistakenly bought in bulk. As a result of this experience, I am Miss Realistic – it's rare that an idea, however good, will see you driving around in a Mercedes wearing Jimmy Choo shoes (mind you, I'm not sure how easy it would be to drive in swanky heels). Sunshine was another problem – it's rare that a British gardener will say this! You'd be amazed how many unexpected items fade in a window display. I now have complete sympathy for the shoe retailers who end up with a range of unmatching suede shoes thanks to displaying one in the window. If I was to ever open a shoe shop, I would make sure it wasn't on the sunny side of the street.

To sum up this chapter in my life, I can say with confidence that retail is tough, lonely and unpredictable. I spent my closed days gardening at an old people's home just to get by – I hadn't built that into my business plan. So why did I close the shop? I suppose it's fair to say that I got bored and broke. In hindsight I wasn't brave enough to be in retail. I'd grown up with my father saying 'If you can't afford it, don't buy it' so I didn't have the bank balance or the nerve to really go for it. Thankfully other opportunities came my way, so this adventure was to end. It wasn't all bad, though. Before, I didn't enjoy solitude, but this was the time that I learnt to cope well with being alone. Being happy in my own company has made my life so much easier moving forward. My retail dream was a bit like owning a soft top car – it was just something I had to get out of my system. It seems wonderful in principle but the reality is a bit different. You might look flashy driving around but you are bound to swallow a few flies and get your hair ruffed up on the journey. Putting a sign up saying 'Closing Down Sale' was one of the hardest things I've done. It might as well have read 'Yes, I failed. All you cynics were right. Please do pop in and rub it in a little further!'

Whilst closing up the shop, the public yet again surprised me. 'What a shame – we loved your shop' was a common quote. To which I wanted to reply – 'So why the hell did you never buy anything?'. Of course, I remained smiling as I packed up my dream into carboard boxes. Fortunately, I didn't live in the town so was spared the torture of seeing the next dreamer move into my old shop (it was later to become a beauty salon and hair removal clinic). If I had lived locally, I'd certainly have invested in a balaclava to try to avoid the sympathetic comments as I walked through town. Once you have escaped the goldfish bowl, you are far better off finding new and distant waters to swim in.

Educating Tamsin

If you were asked to describe a typical college lecturer, how would you do it? I'd reference Frank Bryant – the character played by Michael Caine in the 1983 film *Educating Rita*. Frank wore the same jacket and cardigan day after day, the colour of which perfectly matched his unkept beard. He was slightly upper class but a little rough around the edges, plainly unhappy with his life and an alcoholic. Even with his vices, he always had a certain appeal and there is no denying that he made a difference to Rita's life – and she to his. It's interesting that this is my description of a lecturer because it is no reflection on the wonderful lecturers I have had. There has been the odd beard, but all have been completely sober as far as I can tell.

With this character in mind, when I was asked to be a stand-in lecturer at a horticultural college I was slightly nervous. Actually, I'm lying. I was bloody terrified. The kind of terrified I'd imagine you'd be if asked to enter the sea in a shark cage. There was nothing about my appearance or character that said lecturer. With my annoying habit of agreeing to do most things I am asked (the peril of being a people pleaser), I had found myself giving a one-off practical lecture on bulb planting. I was suggested to the college by someone in the industry. Living not far from the college, I probably seemed a quick solution to a sudden staff shortage. Never in my wildest dreams had I expected to be standing in a polytunnel delivering advice with a few days' notice. It was as unexpected as being picked out of a crowd at a concert by a major pop icon to join them on stage to sing a number. The only concerts I've attended are those by Jason Donovan (when I was the oldest person in the room) and Andy Williams (when I was the youngest). Hardly the ingredients to becoming a rock n' roll lecturer.

Somehow my one-off lecture on bulbs resulted in the day ending with over 60 students in my care for the next year. Why the word 'Yes' came out of my mouth when asked to take on the whole group and an evening class I will never know. Had this 29-year-old been possessed by an alien force or some superpower of the gardening world? It could've been something to do with having just failed to run a profitable shop and my survival instincts had kicked in. Fortunately, I didn't turn to drink or invest in a cardigan to get through, but it was touch and go.

During this time, I learnt as much as the students; possibly more. Most were older than me and, it seemed, with double the brain power of their new tutor. They either had a desire to change their career or simply wanted to improve their own plot and lose the fear of pruning (I've never quite understood the fear of pruning. It rarely leads to the death of a plant). The odd one or two younger students were there because their parents had sent them. I viewed the latter with a great deal of affection as I had been in their gardening boots! These people had set their sights on a qualification and were relying on me to help them. It was time to step up at the same time as putting my head down to get this right. Failure was not an option.

People and their behaviour are as interesting to me as plants. On starting the job, I was given the previous tutor's notes – the folders almost filled the boot of my car. What I'd have appreciated more was a book on how to understand the behaviour of teenagers. How should you react when you're told that the dog has eaten their homework, or they are late because they've been hit by a car yet are miraculously free of any injury? What should I do if they disappeared behind the compost heap to have a fag? Now I'm the mother of a teenager I'm learning the moves and excuses of this age group. Although challenging, to be part of someone's life when they are forming their personality and working out how far the boundaries can be pushed is a privilege. Nothing beats realising that you are getting through to a reluctant learner and helping them to find their feet in the amazing industry of horticulture.

My evening class was to be taught at the local university. University! I'd never in my wildest dreams imagined studying at a uni let alone teaching in one. Uneasy with the workings of an overhead projector I'd arrive with bags and boxes of plants that I'd dug up or pruned from my small back garden. My car was constantly full of twigs, compost, seed trays, reference books and sometimes the odd garden pest. These evening classes were a challenge. The students were often tired, as they'd come straight from a full day at work, and without the inspiration of a garden or the use of a potting bench it was a fairly sterile environment to learn in, so I did everything I could to bring nature to them. After each class I would transform into a cleaner, rushing around the room removing all trace of the after-dark horticultural extravaganza that had just taken place. Teaching horticulture without being in a garden is like cooking without an oven. There was a sign on the door respectfully asking people to 'refrain from eating and drinking in the classroom' so you can bet your bottom dollar that they wouldn't have approved of my trail of compost on the carpet.

Most of my other classes were held at the college and were thankfully of a practical nature. My experience of being a parks gardener was absolutely the best preparation for this. However, before the students and I could pick up our spades my task on teaching days was to master the giant photocopier that lived in the staff room. When I became a horticulturist, I had no idea that I would be consistently faced with office equipment. I'd get to the college at silly o'clock in the morning in the hope that this paper-eating monster was in the mood to work. I seem to have spent my career with my fingers crossed that mowers, leaf blowers and photocopiers would kick into action for me. Prayers were often said as I fed the paper into the feed tray. The words 'paper jam' were my biggest fear. I couldn't possibly let the other lecturers see that I was incapable of using a photocopier. It was bad enough when, just a few weeks into my new role, some clever clogs questioned why I wasn't photocopying on both sides of the paper. Honestly, how on earth was I to know this was even an option? When I was later told that pages could be automatically stapled it nearly blew my mind.

My aim as a lecturer was to convey confidence and disguise my nerves – I'm not an actor but this was the performance of a lifetime. Once my paperwork was in order, I'd regroup in the lady's loo before class began. I'd found a toilet in a Portacabin (these seem to feature in my life!) that no one seemed to go in much. The cabin was officially the Outward Bound centre and was full of canoes and lifesaving equipment. On many occasions I felt as if I should put on one of the life jackets even though I was on dry land. This underused facility became my green room. Leaning on the sink, looking at my reflection in the mirror, I'd repeat the words: 'You can do this. You can do this!' I needed a moment to be alone and practice how I would start the lesson. Enter the classroom too early and the questions would come at you thick and fast, and you'd lose your planned train of thought. It was always best to walk in just on time and be ready to deliver your first line without disturbance. To hold the attention of a class you must be organised, bursting with passion and, most importantly, you must be prepared. Your students need to trust you to learn. At the end of the year they would be sitting an exam. Failure was not an option for them or me – we were all being tested.

This year in my life was to be the most character building of them all, although it certainly wasn't going to be a lucrative one – I now understood why Frank wore the same clothes every day. To teach for about seven hours a week I locked myself in a makeshift office in my garden shed for about 20 hours to prepare. The shed was filled with books I'd begged, borrowed or stolen and they were kept from getting damp with the use of a small oil-fired radiator. The windows were always steamed up to such an extent that I suspect the rumour mill in the street was running high as to what exactly was going on in that shed. To prepare, I crammed like I'd never crammed before. Hands-on lessons were my forte. The technician at the college was my new best friend. Together we faced Ofsted inspections, bad weather and the discovery of unprecedented numbers of vine weevil in the student's nursery beds. She would help me prepare for plant identifications and practical classes and reassure me that we were ready for action. If you've ever been a horticultural student, you'll be familiar with entering the classroom to be met by a row of jam jars, each featuring a twig or two from a plant that needs to be studied for the weekly test. If you are a lecturer, you'll be more familiar with the inevitable comments from students about plant names – I particularly remember a lesson on the shrub *Rubus cockburnianus*! Yes, it is a rude name but I'm grateful for it as it's one that no one ever forgets. Maybe if all plant names were a little cheeky everyone would find plant nomenclature a lot easier.

So, what did I learn? I learned that timing is everything. Being a teacher is like being a comedian – use up all your good material at the beginning of your act and you'll end up with a totally disengaged audience before the end. I also quickly learned never to fudge an answer you're not certain of. This leads to serious trouble and students soon mistrust you. It's so much easier to simply say that you don't know but you'll find out, rather than make up an elaborate story. People respond well to honesty as it makes them feel less ashamed of asking questions. I also discovered that presenting skills are essential – you must tailor your language to the audience. This experience has allowed me to feel at ease when standing in front of a group as a speaker. If I was given the privilege to teach again now, I definitely wouldn't suffer with such nerves. The problem would be the complete reverse. You'd have a job to stop me at the end of the class!

I sometimes regret not continuing to be a lecturer – in hindsight I should've stayed and grown a beard. Being part of other people's horticultural journeys right from the beginning is such a privilege. There isn't anything that compares, and I have never experienced such work satisfaction since. The connection with some of my students continues to this day. On occasion a posse of them turn up as a surprise when I am speaking at events, which is the best compliment I could ever ask for. I wonder if they realise just what that means to me. Life doesn't get better than being the Frank to their Rita.

Naked But Not Afraid

The most wonderful thing about being part of a magazine team is coming up with new ideas. To be honest, most concepts have been around the block a few times – there's nothing new under the sun, as they say – but it's up to editorial teams to put a new spin or another layer of sparkle onto everything to keep the readers interested and the competing titles on their toes. This is a part of the job I adore. I have often been asked by non-gardening friends how on earth you can fill a magazine with just gardening content every month or week. Quite easily, as it happens. When you eat, sleep and live a subject there are always new ideas, advances in practical techniques, fresh gardens and fledgling companies on the scene with new concepts – filling the pages has never been an issue to me. If it was, I'd be in the wrong job.

Perhaps strangely, I positively relish an editorial planning meeting where new ideas are put on the table, chewed over – and often spat out. I use the word strangely as many people dread a meeting of any kind, but not me. After all, sitting in a warm office, clutching a cup of tea and brainstorming with colleagues leaves you very little to complain about. Having worked outside in all weathers I'd call this luxury. I put my enjoyment of such get togethers down to the fact that I have worked on my own a lot in the past and as a result enjoy bouncing ideas off other people – it's like a verbal game of squash: some people win a few points whilst others are knocked off the court. As the ideas get thrown around the room it's great sport to try and pick up what people really think of a feature proposal by looking at their facial expressions and body language. If an idea is received with complete silence, it's safe to say that it's never going to happen. Come up with too many off-the-wall feature themes and your colleagues will stop listening to you all together. The more experience you gain, the more ideas you will knock out of the park. Any suggestion must be practical, affordable and vaguely possible and having been at this for a couple of decades now I'm a past master at what will and won't be feasible. As magazines work so far ahead there is no point coming up with an Easter idea in April, as by then you'll be working on July issues. An out of step calendar is something you must get used to. Christmas is over by September on a monthly title so by the time the festive season arrives you've seen enough of gift wrap and tinsel to last you a lifetime. On many occasions I've been making Advent wreaths and decorating Christmas trees in late summer. The only way around this conundrum is to shoot features a year in advance, but this isn't always possible. In contrast weekly titles work closer to the actual real-time calendar and for this reason there is little room for error – ideas must be quick to turn around. To survive in such a competitive market, weekly magazines need to kick and scream to be noticed on the newsstand as they are often up against thicker and glossier competitors. I'm a great fan of working at a weekly as that constant looming deadline keeps you on high alert – I've always worked better under pressure. There is also more opportunity to cover real life, unfiltered stories and you have the chance to react to current weather and news events.

One of the publishing companies I worked for in the past had its swanky head office in London. The magazine office itself was located on the south coast, where life was much slower paced – by that I mean the actual town and not our colossal workload. On occasion I would head to the city by train to attend a planning meeting. As I stepped through the ultra-modern revolving glass doors at head office, for a moment I became Sarah Jessica Parker. (There is no actual similarity between me and the *Sex And The City* actress, but just humour me for a moment!) On those days, I would find myself dressing completely outside of my usual box, dusting off my briefcase, wearing a pair of heels and inventing an ensemble that looked slightly edgy. One of my failed attempts at trying to fit into the city vibe was an outfit that involved a man's tie and a waistcoat coupled with black tights and short black skirt. Give me a bowler hat and I would have been ready to join the cast of *Chicago*. The heels I often hobbled through the revolving door in were put on just before I reached the building. It wouldn't be unusual to see me leaning against a lamp post or dustbin to change footwear. My feet were littered with plasters the following day but that extra inch gave me a sprinkling of confidence, so it was all worth it, as I'm sure SJP would agree. My high heels are for standing and not walking and as a result they remain in near perfect condition.

Beyond the head office revolving door was a magical world. Just by the way staff dressed you could guess if they were heading to a countryside magazine, women's fashion title, mother and baby, equestrian or music mag. Just like owners are said to come to resemble their dogs, over time it seems that magazine staff become so absorbed by the ethos of their title that they start to morph into who you would imagine the typical reader to be. I am generalising here, but those on the country titles did largely wear tweed and brogue shoes and some even came to work with a gun dog in tow. The fashion magazine staff were likely to be clutching a cup of coffee or hugging a collection of files. (Back in the 90s I'm convinced that files were carried to demonstrate to people how important you were. I had colleagues that would carry folders into work every day, leave them unopened all day and take them back home religiously every night. To this day I have no idea what was in them.) The journalists belonging to the fashion magazines wore effortlessly stylish outfits. A typical look was a cashmere fitted cardigan coupled with a pencil skirt and kitten heels. Often, they would be seen with a divine woollen scarf large enough to cover a single bed draped around their neck and their locks pinned up with a pencil as if they had just shoved it in as they stepped off the tube (however, I suspect it was meticulously placed after hours in front of the mirror).

In contrast, the teams that belonged to the hard-core music magazines were too cool for school, with beaten-up Converse trainers, hair that covered their eyes, tight jeans and t-shirts displaying the logo of a band that I'd never heard of. I expect the gardeners (myself) could be identified by the fact they couldn't walk in their heels and had that 'trying too hard' look – you know, the way in which people dress for a job interview. In hindsight, I should've taken the opportunity to make a statement by wearing a boiler suit and wellies. Maybe if I had arrived truly representing the magazine I was working for and the subject I was passionate about I'd have helped it to be perceived with a bit more interest. It wasn't unusual for people to edge away from me in the lift or in meetings once they'd discovered I was a 'garden writer'. We certainly weren't able to command as much attention and respect as those who worked in the health, home or beauty sector. Us gardeners were definitely the poor relations.

I always enjoyed my trips to head office. It was simply wonderful to see all these magical worlds colliding in one building and just the most marvellous place for people watching. Each title was probably covering the same subjects but with a totally different spin. Take a chair as the theme – the sporting country titles would be filling the pages with upright tweed-covered chairs for the fireside, the music magazines would be likely to cover the delights of a spinning chair that works well in a loft apartment, the women's titles opting for faux fur or Orla Kiely fabric-covered modern chairs and the magazines focusing on cottage and country life would of course be focussing on the best reclaimed and vintage places to park your bottom. Until I'd worked on a magazine I really couldn't imagine how many ways in which you can spin something quite mundane. Now I just adore the many masterful and creative ways that the simple functions and features of life can be made so totally enchanting and tempting. It's pure genius. A visit to head office was sure to get my creative juices flowing and idea after idea would come to my mind but I didn't dare to pitch them all. I had to put forward the one that would get the green light from the editor.

On this particular occasion, the idea that I'd decided was the strongest was to visit a UK nudist camp where I'd heard that the inhabitants had a particular penchant for gardening. The residents lived part time in mobile holiday homes at the camp and shared facilities such as a pool and bar. I can't recall now where I first heard of this place, quite possibly from listening to the radio, but I pitched my crazy idea with enthusiasm. Since my first experience with naturist neighbours I had grown up somewhat and decided that they might actually be on to something. Maybe gardening unhindered by clothes was the ultimate freedom? I was aiming to channel my inner Louis Theroux and get to the bottom of this style of gardening (no pun intended).

Much to my amazement, this bold suggestion was given the go ahead. I was elated but, as with all proposals, actually making it happen was the hard part. My first task was to gain the trust of the residents and get their approval. The second was to find a photographer skilled enough to take shots that would give those featured a little bit of privacy in all the right parts but give the impression that they were naked to the readers.

On the day itself, upon arrival at the camp I sat in the car with the photographer, parked behind a large leylandii hedge, going through the plan for the day. When you have limited time to get your material you must have an action plan. It was vital that we knew which body parts could potentially lead to the magazine being taken off the shelves – get this wrong and my ideas would never see the light of day! Each photograph had to be staged correctly: think *Calendar Girls* and you've got the idea. Strategically placed props and plants were going to be our friends. Going back to the office without enough material to create a feature wasn't an option as there is seldom, if ever, money in the pot to cover a non-story. During this mini planning meeting in the car, it dawned on me that I'd failed to ask the most important question of all. Would the photographer and I be permitted to enter the camp with our clothes on? I had no idea. What a complete fool. This obviously caused some last-minute nerves and emphasised the fact that you really must ask as many questions as possible before arrival at a shoot location, however embarrassing they might be. We eventually decided that we would undress if we absolutely needed to but would walk in confidently and fully clothed. Why, oh why had I not thought of this huge potential issue before? It seemed wrong for my first words on entry to the camp to be 'Do you want us to remove our clothes?'.

Just before leaving the safety of the car, I warned the photographer that we must be professional and not appear shocked in any way. Just as I was delivering my warning, an old man walked in front of the car carrying a pint of milk. He was completely naked and my first reaction was to scream! The photographer looked at me and laughed. It seemed clear I was the one who might cause the embarrassment, not him.

With some relief, the photographer and I were admitted inside the camp fully dressed. Looking around, I could see that all the mobile homes were surrounded by rather wonderful gardens. I had struck gold and discovered a collection of beautifully planted and well-tended plots. Gosh, I was grateful for this! It was far preferable to focus on a dashing dahlia than the naked bodies that accompanied the garden – this wasn't going to be as easy as I'd thought. It's more of a challenge than you might imagine coming up with ways to direct the action without being indelicate! The morning was spent taking shots of bare-bottomed gardeners mowing their lawns or deadheading their perennials and before long we felt the odd ones out in our clothes and became dab hands at asking our willing models to adjust their pose without mentioning their body parts. The only real embarrassment was when we were faced with a couple who had just got back from their weekly shop who were fully clothed. It is the first and hopefully last time I have had to ask someone I am interviewing to kindly remove their clothes.

This visit gave me so much to think about. I was amazed at how quickly I forgot that the residents were naked and began to ask myself why it was such a big deal. I wasn't expecting a trip to a nudist camp to be so thought-provoking. I considered what it would be like to visit our magazine head office and discover everyone naked. It would be almost impossible to pigeonhole people and link them to their interests, work or wealth. Without clothes, everyone is suddenly equal and life might become less competitive. OK, so some of us might have bigger assets than others, but all the trappings of life disappear and you are faced with people as they truly are – it's a great leveller. I'd decided that the whole concept was remarkably cleansing and refreshing. On speaking to these talented gardeners, I discovered that being naked wasn't about showing off their figure. It was about relaxation and escapism. They would get out of their car after a stressful week of work, remove their clothes and relax. The only person on that camp that day that was stressed was me. My photographer was the most laid-back guy anyway, so he was his usual unphased self. To this day I wish I'd dropped my trousers and with them my inhibitions.

The day was rounded off by joining the residents for a drink in the bar and taking part in a game of pool with two gentlemen. The springs had gone in the sofa by the pool table and every time I sat down between turns my face was the same height as the gentlemen's appendages. By this point in the day, though, I was completely unphased by the view. They had normalised being naked.

The feature was very tastefully presented and went down well with everyone from readers to my bosses. I was so pleased by it, because the last thing I'd wanted to do was disrespect the generous people who had welcomed me into their Garden of Eden. Later in the year, I was attending the company's annual awards ceremony and, as we waited to see which celebrity speaker had been booked to open the proceedings and announce that year's winners, the stage showed a picture reel of features that had been highlights of the year. There it was – a slide came up of a man mowing in his altogether. My feature had made the cut. After seeing the photo roll past I picked up my glass of wine and imagined that everyone in the room with me was naked. For the first time, I felt on a level playing field with the journalists from all the hip, cool and on-trend titles. I had proved that gardening, often perceived as the poor relation, was up there, out there and breaking the boundaries.

Baby Changes

During my time as a freelance writer, I feel as if I have tried most things in the way of media at least once. I'm all for giving things a go and never like to turn down an opportunity. Whether or not this is a wise business decision I'm not so sure but it's too late for me to change my ways now.

Since my adventures as a writer began, the world of garden media has changed at a pace. In my thirties I was convinced that advances in technology would never work but now I have turned fifty, I have learnt that I must embrace change even if I don't fully understand it. I am ashamed to say that I never thought that touchscreen would catch on! I now realise that if I don't swim with the tide, I will drown in the water, and no one will be there to save me. Basically, it's a case of dive in or sink to the bottom of the freelance pile.

The most daunting change I have experienced in my career was the move to digital photography, which happened to take place when I was on maternity leave. 'It will never work,' were my words.

On return from my six months off, the working practices of the magazine had completely changed. Even the office kettle had been replaced with a drinks vending machine. Was nothing safe from the clutches of the modern world? The lightbox where we would spend hours looking at transparencies of wonderful gardens with a spy glass was now pushed into the corner. The yellow chinagraph pencils that were once used to mark up the images were now lounging in an unused coffee mug. Images were viewed on screen and could no longer get lost in the post. It was progress but it was about as scary as becoming a mother. The change happened so fast and many of the older photographers didn't have the energy to make the switch – and who could blame them?

Of course, when I say six months 'off' I would like to clarify that going from full time work as a magazine deputy editor to being a mother on maternity leave was far from a break. I don't think I have ever experienced so much pressure before. When you are a driven, career-hungry woman, to suddenly be forced to stay at home and give all your attention to a helpless baby is a shock like no other. I soon found myself at mother and baby groups sitting crossed legged on the floor shaking rattles and talking to complete strangers about when my baby last moved his bowels rather than discussing the latest office politics. For the first time in my life, I was more likely to be found sorting out the sock drawer than planting potatoes (which, I was to discover, is far more complicated with a baby in tow). I found it almost impossible to switch off my deadline-driven brain and focus on nappies, sleep patterns and feeding times. Having a baby is a little like walking through the wardrobe into Narnia and finding yourself in a world that you know nothing about. Some embrace it and others, like me, can't wait to push their way back through the musty old coats and head back to the world they once knew.

I had managed to garden throughout my pregnancy and, near to the end of the ordeal, even moved a rather large delivery of topsoil. This is not to be recommended! What I hadn't appreciated was how hard it would be to garden when my 10lb son arrived. I had visions of happily weeding whilst my baby lay in the pram under the dappled shade of the apple tree. This rarely, if ever, happened. My son was restless and checking on a baby with muddy hands isn't easy. I had hoped that during my six months off I would transform my garden. Not a bit of it. Most of my time was spent driving around in the car hoping to get the baby off to sleep or bouncing around the sitting room to Coldplay in an attempt to entertain him with some popular music. I had learnt that my time was now no longer my own and the garden would have to look after itself. What a relief that plants don't cry when they need attention.

Don't be fooled by those Instagram posts or pictures in glossy magazines of mothers dressed in smocks arranging flowers in a vase whilst their little angel sleeps in the moses basket or wrapped in a papoose around their body. Who are these people and how dare they lead us to think that life with a new baby comes with a soundtrack of birdsong and a room scented with lilac? I won't tell you what the scent of your room is more likely to be! Talking of rooms, if you are lucky enough to have a choice for your nursery, may I suggest that you choose the room with a view over the garden? Believe me, you will be looking out of that window for hours. You will soon have a very good idea of what your garden looks like at dawn, dusk and during the middle of the night.

Another unexpectedly challenging aspect of motherhood for me turned out to be driving the pram (and yes, I do mean driving as I discovered these contraptions can be dangerous modes of transport!). Having absolutely no experience of babies I bought the wrong vehicle, again. I had seen people jogging through the local woods wearing leggings and pushing buggies with thick off-road tyres and I wanted some of that action. Like Delilah, my ill-fated Land Rover, I was seduced by the image in my head. So off I went and invested in a huge pram. I had failed to give a second thought to lifting it in and out of a car and my model was even too large to get through the average sized shop doorway. Living in a market town where most of the shops are in listed buildings, it was almost impossible to enter with my Artic. The pram was useless and never accompanied me on a run – although to be quite honest, I didn't run anywhere apart from to the loo thanks to a now weakened pelvic floor. To resolve the issue of the unusable pram, I eventually invested in a baby backpack. How could this go wrong? Well, let me tell you how. I headed out for a brisk walk with my new mode of baby transport and arrived home feeling as if I had cracked it. Then I discovered a problem. How the hell do you get the baby out of the backpack without assistance? Perhaps one is meant to have a nanny or an army of staff on hand but instead, I was stuck with a baby on my back for a good hour until one of my husband's friends arrived (I'd never met him before) and I was able to ask him to remove the child. My conclusion is that the pram would've been far more useful as a wheelbarrow and my wheelbarrow would've been far more suited to being a pram.

To this day I can't mention that pram to my mother. Once I returned to work, she spent many days pushing it around various horticultural showgrounds whilst I worked. She deserves an RHS medal. At one particular show, the staff room was to the side of the huge building that was home to the giant veg and dahlia displays and had a large internal window so you could watch the action. This is where my mother would make a pit stop on her circuits and I would dash in to breastfeed the baby. Looking back, it was complete madness – without a mother who was happy to admire giant parsnips and prizewinning potatoes for hours on end whilst bouncing a baby on her hip I don't know what I would have done. Every working parent has similar stories to tell, I'm sure. You look back and wonder how on earth you made it from day to day. Just some of the challenges a working mother faces when they return from maternity leave are breasts constantly filling up with milk, complete exhaustion, and an overwhelming feeling of incredible guilt. You limp from one week to the next hoping that your little one doesn't run a temperature or worse, be struck down by vomiting and diarrhoea. Despite all this new stress – or indeed, because of it – I believe that I was my most efficient self during those first few months back at work. When there is no chance of leaving late due to nursery pick-up you work your pretty little socks off to make use of every minute in your day. I was determined to prove to myself that I could do it all and, in order to survive the challenge, every minute of every day away from my baby was to be worthwhile.

I have digressed – on returning to my job I was to face more changes, like the switch to digital imagery. Discovering how fast the world of magazines had changed in just six months made me feel pleased with my decision to go back to work so quickly. Imagine if I had left it a year? I honestly think that I would've walked away in fear or at least been found in the office toilets in tears. Financially,

I had no choice but to go back to work but for that I am now thankful. Yes, my son spent many, many hours in a nursery that probably cost me more than I earnt in the short-term, but making that decision has served me well moving forward. Stepping off the work escalator can make it difficult to jump back on; it is constantly moving. Once on, I have been riding the escalator ever since.

In fact, I could argue nursery fees were worth every penny as the magical team at my son's nursery potty trained him for us. I had attempted to do this over a sunny weekend. I met two other mothers and we decided to spend the day toilet training our toddlers as a group in a garden. It sounded like a great plan but in practice, juggling sun cream, hats, a sandpit and potties isn't easy – more potties ended up on heads than under bottoms. At least I got to spend the day in a garden. That's about all I can say for the success of it!

As my son turned from baby to toddler, he began to be a very useful work accessory. He would appear quite often as the mini gardener in the publication I worked for. His repertoire included collecting snails (a boy after his mother's heart), sowing seeds and pulling petals off my best blooms. And once he could speak the world was his oyster. One memorable time he joined me on a live radio show that was to focus on children's gardening. I spent the journey to the radio station prepping him and he responded like a pro with comments such as 'I love gardening with Mummy.' Once we arrived in the studio the DJ asked him if he liked gardening, to which he replied with incredible confidence: 'No.' The moral of the story is to never ask your kids to help you with your work until they are old enough to bribe with a few quid.

Now a teenager, my son has become my IT expert, my social media consultant and the one person who I will listen to if he says,

'Not such a great idea, Mum' or 'Should you be wearing that?' He is also my companion as I admire open gardens, my shopping partner on trips to the garden centre and the person who records many of my gardening videos. He has spent many hours at country shows and even more hours sitting in a magazine office on a swivel chair patiently waiting for his mum to finish an article. Since his arrival my life has revolved around work, work and more work and I'm convinced that he will be very aware of how important doing a job you love is to life.

By involving him in so much of my day-to-day work over the years, I'd hoped that he would catch the gardening bug. There is only a glimmer of hope at the moment. He is far more involved with plants and gardens than any other teen I know but I don't see a desire for him to make it a career – YET. Although he is happy to help on occasion, the gardening task must never be of any risk to his white trainers or his current hairstyle! Fashion sits firmly above flowers, but I am convinced that a childhood decorated with petals and splattered with mud will eventually result in a deep affection for plants. Even his name is horticultural. Named Herbert Robert he has enjoyed the nicknames of Herb, Herbaceous and Herb Robert (after the weed). He really can't escape his horticultural heritage. I sometimes think that he has taught me more than I have taught him. His presence in my life has given me the skills to multitask, juggle and be prepared for anything.

Motherhood is the most unexpected and wonderful gift – the arrival of children might give your career a little bump in the road to begin with, but your offspring will end up being your main reason to succeed and a very useful way of keeping you tuned in to the ever-changing world that we live in.

The Long Commute

It's rather wonderful that you can have such a good relationship with someone you've never met. Radio DJ Chris Evans was a close friend of mine for seven years and he accompanied me on my morning 50-mile commute. He woke me up, kept me up to speed with floods, traffic incidents and current affairs and got me singing at the steering wheel to the latest hits. And not once did he comment on my tone-deaf attempts. His breakfast show was an essential part of my life. Spending time listening to the radio has always been my way of staying in touch with what's going on in the country and the rest of the world. As a garden writer, I need to be aware of trends and events that might impact the nation. Gardening is connected to and impacted by the weather, the economy, politics and fashion. It's not a profession that can be segregated off from the current issues of the day and you'd be a fool to think that it's just a hobby.

I'd taken a job editing a magazine in Cheltenham, which was a long journey from my home in the Herefordshire countryside.

It was our intention as a family to move closer to the office, but the glittering town property prices put this out of reach. Besides, this job was beyond my wildest dreams and being an editor in charge of a magazine wasn't something I'd ever imagined possible. Surely if I committed to moving the whole thing would go up in smoke? I wasn't going to jinx it.

When the opportunity had come up to apply, I knew that without a degree in journalism or A levels in English my chances were thin. I had nothing to lose, though, and headed to the interview prepared for anything but expecting failure. In the days before I'd spent my time immersing myself in this magazine and going over the competing titles. I even packed a suitcase full of all my previous work to take along. I was as ready as I was ever going to be.

The first interview took place in a hotel, so I suppose arriving with a case might not have seemed that strange. I was delighted to be told I had got through to the next stage, to be held in the magazine offices themselves. A week or so later, on arrival at stage two of the process, I was told straight away that I'd got the job. This was a complete shock and floored me somewhat. I had expected to receive news of my success or failure through the post, giving me time to either cry over the rejection letter in private or leap about the kitchen in excitement. It would also have given me the opportunity to discuss the logistics of taking this role with my husband, who would have to step in and become daddy day care for our young son.

I was told that if I agreed to take the role, my team were ready and waiting to go for a drink with me in the local pub as way of introduction. Without properly thinking through the possible consequences, and without consulting my husband, I said yes on the spot. Most of the best opportunities in my life have arrived out of nowhere and turning down such an offer would've been churlish. Editor's roles on national magazines don't come up very often, so this was probably my one and only chance. The girl who had started her career litter-picking in the parks department was just about to take the editor's seat. Total madness.

The role of editor is vast and varied. You must be a planner, a writer, an HR expert, a budgeter, a people person, a stylist, and a negotiator. This job was going to make use of all the eclectic skills I had collected during my career. This was my chance to share with thousands of readers my love of horticulture. Being given the responsibility of this job absolutely proved to me that it is possible to work your way up from the bottom with the only qualification you truly need: passion. I had somehow weeded and mown my way to the top.

One of the big challenges of the role, apart from getting to grips with management and the day-to-day intricacies of the job, was commuting. Travelling so far each day comes with many problems – expense, danger and exhaustion being just a few of them. Leaving as your child wakes and arriving home as they go to bed isn't something I would recommend. By Thursday, you have a glovebox full of junk food wrappers and petrol receipts and an overriding feeling of jetlag. On Friday, you make a little recovery as the relief and excitement of the weekend ahead gives you a temporary high. There is one advantage to a long commute, however, which is that you have time on your own to plan the day and come up with ideas for the next issue whilst driving. The seeds of many gardening features germinated from behind the wheel of my Mini.

Over the years, I built up a catalogue of disasters on these journeys. Snowstorms, putting the wrong fuel in the car and being stuck in a traffic jam on the motorway for five hours were just some of the trials. On one occasion a flat tyre caused me to pull into someone's drive and later saw me begging to use their toilet as the wait for the rescue vehicle was so long. I suppose I could've peed in the hedge but imagine the headline in the local paper if I'd been spotted: "Gardening Editor Caught Weeing On Wildflowers!"

Every evening I would tune in to the weather forecast as much for my travels as my plants. Ice and snow were a traumatic prospect. If I got to work, would I ever get home? Or would I end up staying in the cheapest B&B in town without a spare pair of knickers to my name? When you're working on a publication, missing deadlines comes with hefty financial penalties to the title, so the team and I often found ourselves risking life and limb to get to our desks.

Before facing the daily challenges of creating a magazine with my team, there was another more pressing hurdle to be jumped. Where to park for free? There were a few spaces at the office, but the car park was like a funnel. If you were in first, you were out last. Those that wanted to see their children before bed needed to park elsewhere as the risk of being blocked in was too high. Back then, there were a few streets in Cheltenham where you might be lucky and slip into a free roadside space. If you're the boss, you can't be late, so time was of the essence (well, of course you can be late but it doesn't set a good example). This was pressure indeed. I'd tried every possible short cut to the office from the many side streets in the town. Having thought I'd exhausted all the options, one autumn morning I had a lightbulb moment.

Leaving the house in the dark that day, I'd tripped over my son's Thomas the Tank Engine scooter. As I drove to work, it struck me. This was it – I had literally fallen upon the answer! The scooter was going to be my saviour. Why hadn't I thought of this before? I'd seen trendy looking yummy mummies scooting through town after dropping their child at school. I was meant to be an ideas person and at the top of my game. I had a BlackBerry (not the fruit – the phone) in my pocket and surely people with such technology should be problem-solving geniuses? I resolved that my new scoot commute would begin the next day.

The following morning, after finding a parking space on the outskirts of town, I put my laptop bag over one shoulder and handbag over the other. The plan was to jump onto the scooter and effortlessly kick and glide my way down the promenade in Cheltenham like an elegant swan, channelling my inner yummy mummy. I'd never tried to ride a scooter before, so this was a test drive. I had not got far at all when I discovered that this mode of transport was less than ideal. Who knew that the handle bars were so low and that the wheels offered absolutely no bounce at all? Every single bump in the pavement was jarring and my wheels quickly got jammed up with autumn leaves. The yummy mummies passed me at speed – their scooters had proper pneumatic tyres and longer handlebars. In contrast, my scooter looked like it was the gift out of a giant Christmas cracker. No wonder my son had dumped it by the back door. The energy required to manoeuvre this useless mode of transport was ridiculous and I soon found myself red-faced with embarrassment and exhaustion. My editor's role had made me very unfit – sitting for hours in the car and then hours at my desk hadn't done much for my physical fitness. Being unfit was just about acceptable, but being stupid wasn't. If you've never been to the spa town of Cheltenham it's a place of beauty, tweed jackets, nice cars and posh houses. It is absolutely not the sort of place you expect to see a middle-aged woman, dressed up for work, on a Thomas the Tank Engine scooter. The yummy mummies might be able to pull it off, but I had to face facts – this was a disaster.

On arrival at work, I hid the offending scooter behind the bins, keen to keep my very bumpy and humiliating ride to work a secret. I already suspected that many people in the building already thought I was a little bit absurd, having arrived at the office a week or so earlier with a chainsaw (one of our articles that month entailed trialling new machinery).

The journey to work had been downhill so the return journey uphill to the car was torture. In an ideal world, someone would have stolen the scooter from behind the bins, but no one was that desperate – in any other town I might have been luckier but not in affluent Cheltenham. I also hadn't considered the added issue of darkness as I headed back to the car, making the bumps and lumps in the pavement invisible and treacherous. On the plus side, I reassured myself, I'd be harder to recognise. With my winter coat flapping in the wind and my back bent low over the handlebars, my silhouette was a dead ringer for the Hunchback of Notre Dame. I eventually arrived at my car, thankful that all my teeth were still intact and relieved that I hadn't been strangled by the straps on my bags. Disappointed that my aim of taking a few valuable minutes off my commute had failed, I threw the scooter back into the garden at home. Nothing ventured, nothing gained. My editor's job relied upon coming up with great ideas but this certainly wasn't one of them!

A Naïve Traveller

S ome opportunities in life should not be passed up, even if they are completely out of your comfort zone and put you on the edge of your seat. A chance meeting had resulted in the offer of a trip to Japan to give gardening lectures. I honestly didn't think that this initial and rather casual conversation would come to anything – I had assumed it to be a nice idea that wouldn't actually happen (I've been presented with many such ideas in my time). But much to my surprise, the initial passing conversation coalesced into a concrete offer of a ten-day trip. Unexpectedly being confronted with the reality rather than the concept sent me into a bit of a spin. This time, it was my friends who persuaded me to grasp the nettle as I was all for ducking out of this once in a lifetime opportunity. As the mother of a young child, I was loath to leave him and the thought of travelling alone and being such a long way from home was a big deal for me. Thankfully, though, I agreed and went on to experience something rather wonderful.

As a gardener, I had never factored in that international travel would be part of my job. I'm far from an experienced traveller and heading so far afield was something I hadn't dreamt of doing. Most of my family don't travel beyond our local market town, and some have only been on a plane once (once was enough for them!) so this was to be a departure for us all. I was leaving my little boy for the very first time and, as the plane took off, I recall that feeling of fear that most parents and guardians are familiar with. What if my son is ill while I'm away? Will he remember me on my return? (I was only going for 10 days so in retrospect this was a little hysterical.) I'm sure many parents ask themselves similar irrational questions when choosing between a work/life opportunity and their child's care. The weight of guilt I was taking on board this flight would certainly have exceeded my luggage allowance! But there I was, on a long-haul flight binge-watching movies and flying into the unknown, eager to experience another culture and another way of gardening. I'm one of those passengers who checks their passport every ten minutes and packs for every possible eventuality. My suitcase is crammed with survival essentials for every situation, with first aid kits, all-weather clothing, every factor of sun cream and emergency snacks being vital travelling companions. I check under the seat to see if the life jacket is there and eagerly watch the flight assistant demonstrate how to put it on. Despite or because of my precautions – who's to say? – the plane didn't drop from the sky or pass through turbulent thunderstorms and we landed neatly in Japan as expected.

For me, this journey was a massive deal, so much so that I had spent much time researching Japanese etiquette, lifestyle and culture, along with learning a few essential phrases – all of which I instantly forgot on landing apart from the vital 'thank you', which is 'arigatou'. I found this word an easy one to remember, as it sounds like my favourite Italian dessert, affogato. This after-dinner treat is simply a blob of vanilla ice cream dropped into a coffee, hence the fact that affogato translates from Italian to English as 'drowning'. Surely having this polite word in my pathetic Japanese portfolio would get me out of a lot of sticky situations and prevent me from sinking?

The thirteen-hour flight was followed by a transfer in a minibus of about five hours. I had no idea if I was actually on the right bus as neither the driver or I had a shared language. 'Arigatou' could only get you so far. As the hours passed, I began to think the journey would go on indefinitely. As I tried to sleep, my head resting against the bus window, I had thoughts of how this journey might end. I decided that I might never be seen again and would be lost in Japan for decades, emerging from a forest as an old woman having discovered unusual and never before seen plants. I would be hailed as an intrepid plant hunter, be top billing on TV chat shows and have plants named after me.

At that point in my daydream, the minibus stopped and the doors were opened. The three other non-English speakers on the bus got out so I followed along with my giant suitcase, assuming that we'd arrived. We hadn't; it was just a pit stop. No wonder the driver had tried to prize my suitcase away from me, but I wasn't letting anyone get between me and my giant traveller's survival kit.

Eventually, in the dead of night, I was dropped off at a train station where I was met by an English-speaking gardener – as usual I had over-dramatized the situation, I would not become a famous plant hunter after decades alone in a forest, and all was well.

On arrival at the hotel, suffering from jet lag and home sickness I sat on the bed and nearly wept as the realisation that I was over 5,500 miles from home hit me (I'd googled that fact before leaving). It was too far for my liking, but I was here now, so I had a word with myself and promised to buck up and get to grips with the situation. This was a once in a lifetime opportunity, I told myself.

It's now over a decade since I went on this trip and my son can't even recall me being away, so more fool me for wasting so much energy wrapped up in guilt and worry. Working parents listen up – in my experience our children benefit from having parents who bring stories home and in turn give them the opportunity to cope without you for a while (although I'd like to add here that I didn't leave him home alone at such a tender age!). I felt guilty about working through most of his childhood, but my son has benefited, I'm sure. Well, that's what I tell myself. I was once told by a working mother that when you have a child you must get used to the feeling of guilt as you can't avoid it. You feel guilty for working as you aren't there for them, and you will feel just as guilty for not working if materially you can't give them so much. So, in short, there is no way out of this parent trap even if you are thousands of miles from home. So you may as well embrace it and get stuck in.

I was joined in Japan by a potter, two fish fryers (I jest – they were in fact excellent chefs from the specialised world of fish and chips) and a bagpipe player who either played the solo in Paul McCartney's 'Mull of Kintyre' or in Rod Stewart's 'Rhythm of My Heart'. I can't for the life of me recall which of those tracks it was, but it was something that had put him firmly on the bagpipe player's map. What a marvellous and randomly wonderful group we were. We had been selected to represent all things British! (The fact that the bagpipe player was Australian was something we chose to brush over.) This group of men, all in their 50s or approaching it, were to make me laugh like I've never laughed before. As soon as I met these characters, I was set free of my worries and started to enjoy myself immensely. They were all seasoned travellers and didn't carry any of the concerns and guilt I had (or if they did, they didn't show it).

My time in Japan was to be spent in a beautiful garden and garden centre, lecturing to students. Days were packed and after 24 hours I had mastered the art of working with a translator. The slightly unnerving thing about having your every word translated is that when you expect a laugh it doesn't come, and when you least expect it there it is. As I presented my view of English gardens and demonstrated planting techniques from the stage in the marquee, the sound of bagpipes could be heard floating across the garden accompanied by the familiar comforting smell of fish and chips. There were some striking cultural differences. I had expected to be bombarded by questions after each talk, but they didn't come. In the UK, gardening questions come thick and fast after every presentation. If I am attending a talk, I see it as the unwritten rule to ask the speaker a question. I'd have to sit on my hands to stop myself. This habit is probably born out of going to a school where students were encouraged to overload their teachers with questions, otherwise you'd risk being accused of not listening. The Japanese show their appreciation and curiosity in different ways. Our hosts were so wonderfully welcoming and enthusiastic about the gardening techniques used in the UK. They even provided me with floral outfits to wear whilst on stage, from their range of own label clothing. Never before had I been even vaguely viewed as an acceptable model, so I was thoroughly delighted to wear their floating rose-patterned outfits.

I was just as interested in their gardening styles and customs as they were ours, and longed to be able to converse with them freely – I couldn't manage to learn French in my years at school so to learn Japanese in less than two weeks would've been pushing it. If I was asked to sum up the main difference between the Japanese and UK gardener, it would be that they are much more patient and more precise with their placement of plants and their pruning techniques. Some of the hedges and trees that we passed in gardens as we travelled to and from the garden centre appeared as if they had been clipped with nail scissors. Our topiary skills certainly can't compete. There seemed to be a common understanding between us all when it came to the language of plants, and they struggle with many of the same issues as we do in our gardens, but their winters take the prize when it comes to the chill factor.

Our accommodation for the stay offered an unexpected treat. At the end of every day, we would go to the Onsen to wash. It was a short walk through the hotel and out into a woodland where the Onsen, or washing facilities, lay in wait. Men and women had separate areas; once inside you would wash in a communal space whilst sitting on a bamboo stool. You would then head outside to take a dip in a cold outdoor bath. Lying in an outside bath in my birthday suit, looking up at the trees decorated with wisteria, is the closest to heaven on earth that I have ever experienced. I was so used to seeing wisteria trained against walls and pinned back like a ballet dancer's bun that it took me quite by surprise to see it growing as it should naturally, leaping freely from tree to tree. It's strange, really, that seeing a plant in its natural habitat should be such a shock. It seems that this bathing ritual and the plants were both just as nature intended.

After washing the worries of the day away we would then head to our evening meal in our robes. No dressing up for dinner, no fuss, just pure relaxation. I wish I had known how this worked in advance of my travels. I had packed a different outfit for every evening, which proved completely unnecessary. On the first evening, after my wash, I had headed back to my room to get dressed for dinner; when I arrived in the dining room I quickly realised that I had made a huge mistake. Everyone without exception was still wearing their robe and slippers. I concluded that other diners would assume that I had not washed. Wearing a robe was an announcement that you were clean – and heading into the dining room in a tight grey dress and red heels was far from acceptable. I looked like the entertainment!

During my time in Japan, I ate nearly everything on offer. I'm a firm believer that even with fish and chips on offer you should try the local dishes, but there are limits. Mine was the very smelly sticky beans. Fermented soya bean is a traditional Japanese breakfast food, said to be very high in protein, but anything that smells that bad wasn't going to pass my lips. After a week in Japan, I never felt healthier – I can't confirm what I actually ate on every occasion and sometimes the dishes would have a flavour that shocked my palate, but the food was out of this world and caused many conversations over the dinner table. I'm sure the lack of bread made me fell lighter on my feet. It seemed that the norm in Japan was to eat little and often. This is something that I have continued to do, especially when gardening. Eating a large meal and then trying to complete a practical task isn't a great idea.

You'll either need a sleep or feel very uncomfortably bloated as you work.

This horticultural excursion was wonderfully rounded off with one night in Tokyo. Knowing that I was unlikely to return to Japan again, my fish frying friends, who were familiar with the city, took me on a night tour of this incredible place. The heat and humidity is my strongest memory, along with the bright lights and the absolute contrast to my life back in Herefordshire. It would be hard to find even one similarity between my home town, where the streets are empty by 4pm, and this bustling metropolis that never sleeps and where the shops seemed to stay open all night. My bed was on the 27th floor of a high-rise hotel. I didn't sleep a wink as I swear the building was swaying. I could possibly put this down to a few too many sakes, however, rather than the movement of tectonic plates.

On arrival at the airport to catch my return flight, I was faced with another naive traveller's conundrum. My suitcase was overweight. Thanks to the generosity of my Japanese hosts, I had been given so many gifts of books, fans and mirrors that my little grey dress and many of my emergency travel accessories were thrown in a bin at the check-in point. Into the bin alongside them went my anxieties and my guilt. I was returning home with a new-found confidence. I could now claim to be an international garden speaker. Imagine that!

Open Season

I t was at a rather boozy dinner party over 25 years ago that I revealed my dreams for the future to friends. Whilst sipping from a fairly large glass of very cheap wine, I explained that I'd like to open a garden to the public one day. This notion quickly caused the conversation to shut down – obviously my dream was unrelatable and of no interest to anyone else at the table. Or perhaps they merely assumed that I was worse for wear and had lost my grip on reality. I've never forgotten how hurt I was that my dream was so quickly dismissed. It's this moment that has made me very cautious when being presented with someone else's career aspirations – no one should be a crusher of dreams. A quarter of a century since I shared my deepest desire at that dinner table, it is now my day to day reality. For nearly ten years now I have been running an open garden in Herefordshire with my uncles and sister, so dreams do come true. On some days, of course, it's a case of be careful what you wish for – not long before sitting down to write this

I was giving a fresh coat of paint to the walls behind the urinal in the gent's toilets!

Stockton Bury, where I garden, doesn't belong to me, although I have a strong emotional attachment to it. The country garden and I have history as I lived in the house it belongs to with my grandparents when I was sixteen. I would watch my uncles, Raymond and Gordon, working away on their creation and marvel at the results. During the time I was there this gave me much entertainment – that, and trying to perfect moves from *Dirty Dancing* in front of the mirror in my bedroom.

To create a garden from scratch and be young and enthusiastic enough to then turn it into a business is an almost impossible task. Gardens take time to mature and until they have that settled and slightly aged look they are rarely of interest to the paying public. In the meantime, the gardener ages too! Fortunately, my uncles started their garden in their prime of fitness so can now welcome people to their mature plot and witness the pleasure it brings to so many. I fear for privately owned open gardens in the future. There are so many that are teetering on the edge because a younger member of the family has failed to step in in time. Usually, gardens are created out of love and passion rather than considered from the beginning as a business. They are rarely profitable and can seldom support more than one household. If you take on such a challenge, you are probably the type of person who would marry for love and not money! Nevertheless, I compare a garden that will appeal to a wide audience to an old leather chair. Such a chair has a story to tell and has been improved over the years by use. The well-worn leather offers comfort, character and intrigue – as does the garden at Stockton Bury.

The daily workings of an open garden are far more about
people than plants, and challenges that I would never have
considered relevant often present themselves. Believe it or not, it's
hard to make time to garden with all the other shenanigans that
need taking care of. Marketing, taking bookings, planning menus,
window cleaning, learning to be a barista, brushing up on first aid
and event planning are just a few of the added duties. That's just
in the quiet times. Gardening once open season is upon you is
almost impossible. The temptation to enter into conversation with
a visitor instead of tackling the border is great. This will explain
why you might just catch a glimpse of my bottom from under
a shrub if you visit. I sometimes seek out-of-the-way corners to
weed where I hope to go unnoticed. If you employ a gardener to
help you it's to your advantage to find someone who doesn't relish
the idea of long conversations, otherwise they'll achieve next to
nothing. It's not that I don't want to talk to our visitors – those
who have met me will know that it's hard to stop me talking. It's
simply that you must strike a balance and ensure that the garden
itself gets some of your attention. I often think of working in the
garden when it is open as being comparable to hosting a party. You
can't sit in the corner chatting to one guest, however enchanting
they might be – you must work the room and keep everything
flowing. That pyramid of precariously displayed Ferrero Rocher
chocolates needs to be shared out!

If you have ever sold your house and have had the experience
of keeping things tidy for prospective buyers, you'll have faced a
little bit of what we go through in the garden every day. The weekly
washing can't be left on the line and all trip hazards need to be
removed before the gates open. Even inside the house should be

kept in good order as people often peer through the windows. When my uncle first opened the garden, I recall people looking through the window as we tucked into our Sunday lunch. It was so strange at the start but now it's odd when there isn't anyone looking around. And I must admit I'm guilty of staring through windows too when garden visiting – the temptation is just too great. It will serve me right if I ever catch a glimpse of something I'd rather I hadn't!

Before opening time every day there are essential tasks that must be done. Toilets must be in tip top order and any bird poop removed from garden benches. No one wants to sit in faeces on a day out – you don't want your visitor to remember your garden for that! Having worked in a public park I have put my hand in my fair share of poop and I am a master at identifying which animal it comes from – a rare talent, I know. Worse than that is if there is a death in the garden overnight (not a human death, I hasten to add). If a fox has feasted on a rabbit in the night, all traces of this meal must be removed. Visitors have come to see the softer side of nature and not the blood and guts.

I find that what tends to happen to me is that the garden and the facilities are spick and span, but as the bell strikes eleven I appear at the reception desk looking like a wild woman with no care for self-presentation. Every year I promise myself that I will dress to impress the visitors and appear effortlessly elegant, like a picture-perfect gardener. I intend to welcome them in a pair of practical yet stylish dungarees, my hair tied in a messy bun, perhaps with a headscarf, and wearing funky gardening boots – you know, just like the women you see carrying baskets of home grown veg in magazines such as *Country Living*. However, I have searched for dungarees of this kind and nearly fallen flat into a pile of compost in shock as to the ethically produced price. I have also tried growing my hair long to create an effortless bun. Unfortunately, the result was that I looked more like a retired ballerina or – as my uncle kindly pointed out – like one of my spinster great-aunts who have long since passed away. In the pictures I've seen of them they look very austere, so I'm not sure if this is a compliment. I'm also convinced that when my hair is up it adds a few centimetres to my nose. The upshot is that my hair has been cut and I have given up on the possibility of somehow looking effortlessly gorgeous in a bun. The reality is that I will be dressed in old jeans, a very unflattering bobble hat (to hide the bad hair) and a jumper that has been handed down to me by my son. He is now sixteen, over six-feet tall and I refuse to give away the perfectly good clothes he claims to have grown out of. If you see me wearing Nike then don't be fooled into thinking I'm a fitness fanatic – no, I'm simply a thrifty mother. This thriftiness and determination to use his hand-me-downs has led me to an excellent discovery, though: rugby skins are the best undergarments for us gardeners. I spend so much of the summer standing in our stone reception area, which never gets warmer than about 15 degrees, that you will never see me in short sleeves or with a tan.

Lunch breaks are impossible when we are open so don't be surprised if you catch me trying to subtly eat a bag of Frazzles with very muddy fingers at the potting bench. This bench is located in our reception area and doubles up as a desk for writing and a place for pricking out and potting on. I know I should be eating carrot sticks or such like, but I can't resist a bit of junk food – crisps are my weakness. The exception to this rule is the month of June, when my crisps are replaced with a lunchbox full of cold cooked broad beans from the garden. I can hear the happy chinking of cutlery from our café and smell the freshly baked cakes and bread, but the café team are far too busy to worry about a queue-jumping gardener so I must come armed with my own lunch. If I hang around the door looking forlorn like Oliver Twist, though, I'll sometimes get the wonky brownie or the scone that's too small.

Very few people have any idea what is involved in opening a garden – and why would they? Some assume that it's simply a case of dusting off the open sign and switching on the coffee machine in the café. The reality is that it takes a whole six months to get the garden ready to open again in time for spring. So, why on earth would anyone do it? To be honest, I have asked myself that question time and time again, but recently I've found the answer. During 2020 and the Covid-19 pandemic, we decided not to open and that was when the reality of having this space to ourselves hit us. It suddenly became very clear why we spend hours with brush, rake and trowel preparing for visitors. Not having guests was devastating. It seemed almost pointless working in the garden but not being able to share it. I mean, why get your hair cut if you aren't going out? We missed the laughter, the constant gardening chatter and even the trail of tissues that visitors often leave around the garden (why, I know not!).

Our visitors become friends and the garden is a special place to so many people – a sanctuary where they know they will be welcome and feel safe. Over the years, I've found that the garden has become less about what iris is growing in the right-hand corner by the pond and more about relaxation, escapism and community. When at last we opened after that enforced break of a year so many people expressed their complete joy at being able to return to their special place. Sadly, though, it wasn't unusual for people to return without their partner, sibling or friend; they had been taken by the pandemic. The reality of what we had been through was suddenly very evident and overwhelmingly heart-breaking. Many had returned to be in a place that held so many happy memories of their loved one. It brought home to me the true value of what we do here. In its own special way, the garden at Stockton Bury offers therapy, and this strengthens my view that everyone can get something out of spending time in a garden, even if they profess to having no interest in the physical art itself. It's not unusual for people to be unexpectedly moved by the garden and leave in tears. Being immersed in plants can leave you overwhelmed.

When I first started work at Stockton Bury the typical visitor was a plant enthusiast with far more knowledge than I could ever dream of acquiring. Having got used to my uncle being the person at the reception for the last 25 years, it was a surprise to many visitors to be met by a woman. Sometimes, I felt as if I had returned to my days in the parks where my presence was almost shocking. Many assumed that my uncle must have died as there could be no other possible reason for being so rash as to replace him for a few days a week with a 'girl'. I was once asked 'Can you fetch someone who knows about the plants, please?' This was spoken before I had even muttered a word. At the time I was in my early forties. It made me wonder how old some gardeners think you must be to know anything at all. Fortunately, this attitude seems to have changed over the last few years – or perhaps I have just got more acceptable as I've aged!

Speaking of age, I have also noticed that the average age of our visitors has dropped. This is exciting and has encouraged us to further think outside of the 'open garden box' and put on events such as pilates or yoga amongst the plants. If you'd have asked me ten years ago if people would have been exercising in Lycra on the main lawn, I'd have laughed. Now I think it's amazing when I see people clad in exercise gear heading into the garden.

The number of gardening questions I have received in recent years has also noticeably reduced. People seem suddenly more content to photograph mystery plants and look them up when they get home. The mobile phone has definitely changed the garden visiting experience. In years gone by, being asked to name 'a plant with green leaves at the far end of the garden' was nothing unusual but now I'm almost always shown an image on a screen. When buying plants from our small nursery, the customer will search the internet for the plant they are eyeing up and make the decision themselves as to if it is suitable for their plot. I suspect that in the next few years plant identification apps will do all my work for me: visitors will simply be able to point their phone at a plant and its vital statistics will be revealed. Is this progress? I'm on the fence – being able to converse about plants is all part of the fun. If enthusiastic gardeners start to feel that they don't need an expert on hand, it would seem a shame to me.

I am still frequently asked what week the garden is at its very best, but I really struggle to answer this question. I feel unfaithful to the season we are in if I pick another. The truth is that this is an impossible question as every month has its merits. It's like asking someone which one of their four children they prefer. With social media being a priority for many, I am now more likely to be asked 'What day exactly should I come to see the wisteria?' rather than 'How do I prune it?' The former is so much harder to answer as flowering time is dependent on weather and, however hard I have tried, I just can't control that.

Weather is obviously a big issue for this type of business. The last thing I do every night before I hit the pillow is to check on the forecast for the following day. My sister, who makes the all-important cakes for the café, is also glued to the weather forecast. Too hot and people won't come, too wet and they will head to a well-covered garden centre instead. You need a still, mild but sunny day for successful footfall. It always surprised me that people seem very sensitive to weather; out in all weathers myself for work, I find it quite hard to fathom. If I plan to go and see a garden the threat of rainfall will rarely defeat me. In fact, some of my best garden visits have been in the rain – you get the garden almost to yourself that way.

At the end of every open season in September our customers wish us a premature 'Happy Christmas' and we shut the gate until spring. Many assume that it's then time for us to put our feet up but alas, far from it. For six months I have ignored the housework in my home and the cobwebs are calling. As well as tending my own neglected place, the autumn and winter are times of hard graft in the open garden. When you are showing off a plot there is no time to rest on your laurels. We need to keep the garden match fit and on point. Another layer of clothing goes on over the rugby skins and we start the preparations for the following year. In the words of the manager of Kellerman's, from my favourite teenage film *Dirty Dancing*, 'We have shared another season of talent, play and fun'. I'm still waiting for someone to teach me how to do the Mambo but for now, I'll stick to manoeuvring around the lawn with a spring-tine rake.

Hands On

Is it fair to say that there are people that do and people that don't. By that, I mean that some are more than happy to pick the greenfly off their lupins and turn the compost heap with their bare hands and others would find the mere idea simply revolting. Does this fear of dirt, insects and garden gunk put them off gardening? I suspect it might. It is for this reason that I advocate we all roll round in mud as children, as with the mess comes lots of magic. Fortunately, I have grown up surrounded by muck tumps, chicken poop, sheep droppings and people that do. My family are hands-on practical types with not a squeamish one amongst them. They are more likely to be found leaning on a broom than a desk.

My grandmother was truly remarkable and was always on the go. During my childhood she hand-washed clothes, made her own butter and strained the milk from the cow through a muslin. We always were the last family to take on any advances in technology, and still are today. I recall my grandfather being very cynical about the idea of having a freezer. I seem to have inherited his unease of white goods and am still to be convinced that a dishwasher has any use!

I don't ever recall my parents sitting down to watch the television and I grew up with the concept that if it was light outside there was work that could be done. Their free time was spent breeding – ponies, rabbits and chickens in large quantities! My sisters and I would spend many hours helping Dad fix fences or build things, so we got rather adept at running to fetch tools and holding the ends of pieces of wood. At the time, I'd rather have been lying on my bed looking longingly at my posters of Morten Harket but there was no getting out of 'Dad's weekend projects'. My mother, on the other hand, spent our childhood weekends cleaning out hen houses in a boiler suit and head scarf – she was always covered in feathers and usually had a gaggle of geese or hens following behind her. This excellent grounding in mucking in and mucking out has been a godsend for my work as a gardener. The skills picked up along the way have given me the tools to be reasonably practical. As a child I turned my hand to building drystone walls, attempted woodwork and I made some pretty awesome garden dens. All of which I would argue are essential skills for a future gardener.

My Uncle Raymond, who has created Stockton Bury Gardens with his partner Gordon, has also been a great inspiration to me. His work ethic is off the scale. Now in his mid-seventies, he continues to be very active – he is the ultimate hands-on person. There is literally nothing this man can't do. His large workmanlike hands proudly bear the marks of all his labours. Raymond was born at Stockton Bury and has never strayed very far from it. From him, I have learned that gardens aren't created overnight and the more you know the soil and the local weather the more successful you will be. He knows every inch of his garden and he belongs to it as much as it belongs to him. As we work in the garden and watch the skies change overhead, Raymond can predict the weather heading our way with remarkable precision. If you were to offer him a royal palace and garden in exchange for his plot, I can guarantee you that he wouldn't be interested. Nothing, absolutely nothing, would entice him to leave this place. It would be easier to persuade Peter Pan to fly away from Neverland. He won't even leave the place for a holiday. Days off and holidays are an alien concept to him.

Those who have visited the garden will know Raymond as the man in the shorts and wellies – he is famous locally for his unrivalled sense of fashion and his bright red Land Rover. If his very weighty steel toe-capped wellies are outside the back door, I know he is inside having coffee, accompanied by a side dish of very large chunks of cheese. If his boots aren't there, goodness only knows where he will be but one thing is for sure, he won't have gone far from the farm or garden. He recently treated me to a pair of these safety wellies and although I value the idea of my toes being safe it's a little like wearing shackles. I wonder if this was his attempt to ensure I don't hot-foot it off the place?

When in the garden I can hear him coming as his wellies click against his bare legs. This clash of flesh and rubber is my early warning system that he is en route. I fully expect to be told that what I am doing is wrong. He has an easier, more tried and tested technique for most gardening tasks. I long for the day when I have a better method than him! Overwintering dahlias is a classic example. In my first year at Stockton Bury, I spent time titivating my tubers by placing them upside down in trays. As I worked away in the cellar with my tubers (this is our wonderful frost-free storage place) Raymond literally flung his tubers over my head and they landed on the floor. There they stayed until spring, untouched by human hands. His dahlias overwintered better than my pimped-up specimens. From this and many other examples of Raymond's 'instinct' gardening I have learned that we all fuss far too much about our plants. He has also proven to me that you can't learn about gardening just from books (not the best things for a gardening author to admit, but I am nothing but honest). You need to garden your own way to suit your energy levels, your fitness, your time-frame and your mood. Step-by-step instructions that involve all the kit and caboodle are all very well but are sometimes that step too far. He is the master of his garden and having gardened here before he wore long trousers (well, actually we are still waiting for that to happen!) he is pretty much self-taught.

So, what's it like working so closely with family? Far and away the best thing is hearing all the stories of the past. Knowing when the cider press at the farm was last used and the name of the pony that worked it adds historic magic to the place. Every day I am immersed in our family history and it makes me fall ever deeper in love with the garden and farm. I had no idea until recently that the watering cans with short spouts that can be seen in the garden were used by my great aunts to carry water up the stairs to fill their bath. Having this knowledge turns them from just a cluster of dented old cans into family heirlooms. The large metal containers where our herbs grow were once giant cooking pots used by my great aunts to cook enormous stews that they shared with others in the village. They look more like cauldrons to me. Although I only remember one of these aunts, it's obvious to me that they were also fine hands-on types. Having said that I love hearing these stories, on occasion Raymond will choose the most inappropriate moment to share. As a coachload of people arrives at the garden he will often pick this exact time to tell me about a farming technique of yesteryear. 'Not now,' I will say as I rush to greet my guests.

Raymond's daily stories of the past are a constant reminder of how fast the world has changed and also how affectionately he holds these memories. As a boy, he would deliver the coal to the school with the gardener using the pony and trap and drop off the candles at the church for Sunday. He often tells me how he set to work on the farm in the school holidays (this explains why leisure time is a concept he can't grasp). This all sounds like something from Dickensian times, but it wasn't. It's no wonder that he is shocked when he sees a visitor paying their garden entry by using their phone. I wonder how people will be paying by the time I reach my seventies? Maybe we will just have to wink at a credit card machine to buy our plants in the future?

There is a downside to being in a place filled with so many reminders of the past: many of our gardening tools also hark back to the generation before. Raymond is a believer that if it has a blade and can be sharpened it still has life in it. This is debatable. After struggling to cut through branches with a pruning saw that could quite easily have been used by Lady Chatterley's lover, I long for something a little sharper and lighter. (Alternatively, I might settle for a little help from my own gamekeeper-gardener!)

Pretty much everything at Stockton Bury is from the place or of the place. Very little has been bought by Raymond and very little is wasted. He is a master of recycling. Old harrows are turned into gates in his forge, an old mantelpiece transformed into an auricula theatre. If you can't buy what you need in our local town or find it lying about the place, then we simply can't have it. Seed is saved for the following year, plums are stewed and frozen (bags and bags of them – the freezer looks like a blood bank!), terracotta pots are stuck together with glue if they break, and bailer twine is used to fix or hold up pretty much everything – including my trousers! When Raymond recently went through his wardrobe, he was keen for me to adopt his 1980s white jacket (now rather yellowed) with roping details, rather than throw it away. It looks like it might have belonged to Freddie Mercury! You might be relieved to hear that you won't ever see me in this jacket, as I politely declined. It remains in Raymond's wardrobe. It will end up on a scarecrow before he has the heart to throw it out.

It will never be possible for me to become as entwined with a place as Raymond is as I've moved about too much and don't have enough years left under my bailer twine belt. I'll just settle for being a tiny part of the past and present of his garden. Who knows, maybe in the future I will be the one trying to dress my younger relatives in an aged garment from my wardrobe. Come to think of it, I do have a red leopard-print catsuit somewhere. I think I'd better look it out.

Questions, Questions, Questions

I've developed a theory that some people think that gardening information should be given out for free. This has happened to me time and time again throughout my career. It's partly my own fault, as I am the world's worst at being brave enough to price my work and advice. If I attempt to charge what I would describe as a reasonable price for a garden consultation, I will often get the look that clearly says 'Who the hell does she think she is?'. If you undercharge, though, your client will have no respect for you at all and you will be perpetuating the myth that advice should be free.

There is and always will be a desire for gardening advice and for that I am thankful. Inquisitive minds are what push the boundaries in gardening. How exactly experts provide answers has changed incredibly over the years but the challenge of turning this type of work into a living still remains one of life's great mysteries. No one should be deterred from asking a question, but they should consider when, where and how best to pose it. Not all situations are equal! On one memorable occasion on a dark winter's evening,

I was invited to dinner at a friend's new house. My husband was unable to come but they insisted I came anyway – I was soon to find out why. They had gone to the effort of putting temporary spotlights in the garden in the hope that I would be able to design their plot whilst they served the starter. When the curtains were pulled back and the spotlights switched on, I was half expecting a troupe of dancers to appear in the garden as the evening's entertainment. No such luck. I might not always receive payment for my experience, but I have been treated to some rather lovely meals. There is, after all, no such thing as a free dinner.

When I opened my garden shop word quickly raced around town that a gardener had arrived in the vicinity – not just any old gardener but one who was trapped behind a counter with no means of escape. In my time I have been asked all sorts of garden questions, from identifying a mystery leaf to wanting me to design an entirely new garden for a school complex. It wasn't at all unusual for people to arrive at the shop with photographs of their garden and expect me to create a brand-new design for them in an instant. These people were never known to me as customers. One wonders if they would dare ask an interior designer to throw together a scheme for their lounge or a vet to diagnose their pooch's pains for nothing? Alas, I'm not a designer so the disappointment when I didn't suddenly reveal an all-singing all-dancing coloured and scaled drawing was clearly obvious. I might be a competent gardener but I'm not a magician.

Houseplants are often the source of many panicked questions from friends via WhatsApp or text message. 'HELP! My diffenbachia is drooping!' This is where the tables are turned, and I start to question them. How much light is it getting? Have you overwatered? When it comes to houseplants, it's always a process of elimination to get to the root of the problem. I'm afraid that I'm one of those gardeners who might, on occasion, encourage you to give up on a plant. There is absolutely no point weeping over a specimen that is never going to recover. Life is too short and with so many other fantastic plants to try I might just advise you to move on. Compare plant ownership to speed dating. Give the specimen a little time to prove itself, assess if it will fit into and enhance your life and if it won't – move on. It might not be the answer people want but I'm not afraid to give it.

Something that bugs me more than being asked questions is not being asked questions. Yes, I know that makes me sounds as if I'm never happy but read on. There is nothing worse than being part of a Q&A panel and being passed over. I started doing charity Q&As when I was fairly young and most of the questions would be aimed towards the older gentlemen on the panel. I will agree that those with many years of experience under their belt do usually have more experience of problem-solving but younger gardeners can often add a new perspective. I soon learned to jump in with my own little quips and forged my own way. There is always more than one answer to a gardening question, so my view was just as relevant as anyone else's. I often wonder if I should attend such events with soil under my nails just to emphasise the fact that I'm not just a keyboard gardener.

When and where you are asked questions can also be a cause of entertainment. I have been told by male gardening experts that they have even been asked questions about pruning whilst at the urinal. My most extreme questioning experience was at Stockton Bury, the open garden I look after with my uncle. A customer came flying into the plant sales area to tell me that they thought their partner had died in The Dingle (he hadn't – far from it, thankfully). Panic set in and I grabbed my phone to call an ambulance. Fortunately, the paramedics were with us in minutes and as the vehicle pulled into the drive, with flashing light and sirens, I raced towards it. It was at this point that a lady approached me with her mobile phone: on it was an image of a seed pod she wanted identified. (I later established that the image was of a plant that wasn't even in our garden but somewhere she had visited earlier in the week.) Now this story is a source of entertainment to me, but at the time it was on the verge of being horrific. Hadn't she seen the ambulance and the sheer look of terror on my face? I certainly wasn't in a fit state to answer her. It was a magnolia seed pod, if you were wondering, but I wasn't about to tell her that.

With the arrival of social media and mobile phones I find I am experiencing slightly fewer questions on common plants from visitors to the garden. Often they will message me later through Instagram instead with their photo, or do their own research online. I have to confess that, at the start of the open garden season, I will have got out of practice and over winter many plant names will have left me. The hardest and most regular question of all to answer is 'Do you know of a gardener who would come and help me? Someone who knows what they are doing?'. If this is being asked by an elderly customer, my heart melts. I know how important it is for them to find an experienced person who will help them to keep their garden. So often they have been widowed and their children do not live nearby, so they are left looking out of their kitchen window at a garden that is getting out of control. The sad truth is that there is a terrible shortage of knowledgeable gardeners – many of the experienced ones have chosen to take work as head gardeners at larger properties to secure a regular income. If you are lucky to have competent self-employed gardeners about, you'll be waiting forever as they are so busy. If I had the power to answer just one gardening question it would be this one, as I know it causes such distress. Apologies if you are now weeping into the pages of this book but this is a sad reality for so many older people.

Being asked constant questions isn't all bad as it has saved me from being at the hectic till point in our garden café. My sister who runs it simply can't bear it when I'm asked how to prune something when the queue for coffee is out of the door. It's for this reason that I'm often sent to the sink to do pot-washing, where I can't cause any hold-ups with my gardening chit chat! The only blockage I'm in danger of causing there is if a tea bag gets jammed in the plug hole.

Talking the Talk

As the evenings draw in and the roads get icy, enthusiastic experts start to spread their passion for gardening across the land. Those that have the bottle, the brains and a reasonably reliable car offer talks to garden clubs, Women's Institutes, U3A (University of the Third Age) and local groups; both to subsidise their gardening pay and for the pure pleasure of it. The venue for these talks is nearly always a village hall in the middle of nowhere and travelling to each event is like taking a mini adventure into the unknown. More often than not, talks are held in the evening and I can often return home just before midnight. Without fail I will have something entertaining or unexpected enough to share that justifies waking up my husband to communicate it with him. God forbid I arrive home any later than twelve and risk my husband realising that I'm not in fact a princess! He will listen with one eye open and pretend to be interested about the events of the evening, but his late-night acting skills don't always convince me.

Gardening can be a solitary career choice, so getting the chance to talk about your first love with other enthusiasts can be as good for the speaker as the audience. On occasion, I have certainly witnessed speakers enjoying the event far more than their audience and ignoring the signs of boredom displayed by those listening. Although it's my job as a speaker to keep everyone bright-eyed and bushy-tailed, I've learned not to be offended by the odd person who falls asleep. I try to reduce the chances of this occurring by keeping at least one light on. Plunge the room into darkness to show off your slides and you are doomed. I speak from experience having been in the audience at one talk that followed a wine and cheese spread, and found myself the only one awake when the lights came on!

Timing is everything. It's very unnerving for the group if a speaker dashes through the door at the last minute. Arriving in plenty of time avoids putting everyone's nerves on edge – including your own. There is nothing worse than trying to set up your screen and projector in front of an already seated audience. It's a bit like being watched while you're cooking. I'd far rather my guests only saw the plated meal and not the mess I make in the kitchen! Another important timing issue is keeping it concise. Overrunning as a speaker is, as far as I'm concerned, a sin. There are often members boiling kettles and laying out teas, eager to have their moment once your last slide has been shown. No one enjoys a speaker who is so fond of their own voice that they drag on into the night with not a care for those who are ready with the tea tray or eager to go home to bed. Rambling on indefinitely is lazy and shows a lack of preparation. You are better off leaving them wanting more than with a memory of a dull night and a pained posterior – village halls are not often known for their comfortable seating.

Compromise and consideration for others is vital if you are going to be a success on the circuit. You need to be able to quickly adjust your talk to suit the group – some love a bit of a joke whilst others might look over their glasses at you in disgust. You need to quickly work out which type of group you are speaking to by testing the water with a gentle bit of humour. Somewhat counterintuitively, you also can't assume that everyone in the room is in a position to garden. Some will have downsized and now have only a few pots whilst others will have acres and a gardener to assist. The art of giving a good talk is making it diverse enough to suit absolutely everyone.

There seems to be a general perception that doing a talk is easy and only justifies a minimal fee but after treading the boards for a few years now I feel strongly that clubs get what they pay for. Good speakers need to charge a reasonable price as they are putting on a performance each time. Holding a room of people's attention by yourself for an hour takes practice and skill; it's a big responsibility. You also must be prepared to answer any question that is thrown at you and there is always someone (usually an ex-teacher) who is determined to catch you out. It doesn't matter if you are speaking to ten people or to a hundred – the preparation is just the same. I've come a long way since I gave my first talk all those years ago. Many mistakes have been made but by making them I have learned my craft. I now feel very much at home in front of an audience. This is strange really, as I'd never in a million years take part in a play on stage. The thought of pretending to be someone else fills me with dread. I only know how to be me.

To put on a show, preparation is to be taken very seriously. It reminds me of the packing for a Duke of Edinburgh award weekend (I've never done such a crazy thing, but I was quick to send my son off with a rucksack that weighed more than he did). You need a survival kit for a talk – really, you do. I never leave home in the winter without a paper road map as back up for the satnav, as I often find myself in such remote places that digital devices won't connect when I most need them. I also always pack a flask of tea, sandwiches, blanket, paracetamol, a spade (essential to dig yourself out of a snow drift) and that's all before you add in the screen, projector, computer (plus a back-up computer), extension lead, props and a lipstick. If I had one, I think I'd even take an emergency flare. As age has crept up on me, I have become a catastrophiser (I suspect this is a side-effect of the onset of the menopause). I will often be spotted in a layby a few miles from home double-checking the contents of my boot for the fourth time. Sometimes I wonder if I was stopped by the police, what they would they make of finding a spade in the vehicle. Now that would be a story worth waking up my husband for! It's never the talk that gives me the nerves, it's the equipment. Imagine forgetting your HDMI lead? What if the bulb goes on your projector? My absolute dream is that a club has all the kit and I just need to waltz in and whip a memory stick out of my pocket.

Fortunately, one thing I can get away without packing is a microphone and speaker. I have a loud enough voice that they're usually quite unnecessary. I was once talked into buying what I can only describe as a boogie box speaker that came with a headset microphone – when I went to collect said speaker from the shop, much to my astonishment I saw that it also came with a set of disco lights built in. When I tested it, it whistled and gave my voice a delay, so I was spared the embarrassment of walking into a hall looking like a teenage beat-boxer and it now sits in the corner of my kitchen gathering dust, giving the impression that I was once a super cool DJ. There's only been one event where this piece of kit would've been in keeping with the setting. There was an issue with the intended hall, so my talk was moved over the road to the working men's club. I had to compete with a kid's party in the next room where Kylie Minogue was suggesting that we all jumped to the beat, a juke box that would occasionally rattle out a random tune and the usual carryings on of a busy bar. I shouted out advice about how to store dahlias over winter whilst wearing a tweed jacket. This event was memorable in many ways, but also confirmed that if I could be heard against that background noise there was no need to invest in another microphone.

There is an art to arriving at a hall looking unflustered and organised. Parking in the right place is vital. I tend to arrive early and park in a dark and distant corner of the car park (this might appear a little dodgy, but I like to sit quietly with my tea and be able to apply my lipstick without an audience). Once I'm looking refreshed and ready to rock, I'll move the car closer and ensure that I pick a spot where I'm not going to be blocked in. If refreshments are offered after the talk, you're in danger of being penned in for hours. Planning an escape route is vital, especially if you have a long journey home.

Deciding what to wear is another important consideration. Will I need a vest and polo neck, or will the hall have overhead, electric heaters that are the equivalent of being toasted under a grill? I like to be smart but look practical, and I tend to wear one item that offers a flash of colour in an attempt to keep the audience awake. I'm always in trousers and normally a pair of highly polished long boots (not over the knee boots – that would be taking it too far). I can't abide speakers who turn up looking like they've just dragged themselves off the sofa. This is a job that you are being paid to do so your audience deserve a smart presenter. After all, it's not often that you are being looked at intensely for a full hour. On occasion I will attend a talk and sit in the audience. I love to hear the whispers. 'Jean, have you noticed he has a hole in his jumper?', 'Barry, can you hear anything?', 'I do wish the speaker would stop leaping around, it's making me dizzy.' 'Who is this person they have booked for tonight – I've never heard of them, have you, Margaret?'

When the speaker is someone well-known who has been on TV, all the front seats are filled quickly, whereas when I do a talk the front seats often remain empty. I notice that it's often a man who gets the crowds in. The majority of groups are made up of women and a young male speaker will see them sitting on the edge of their seats in silence. Until, that is, they get the chance to ask a question, when a sea of hands fly up with the same enthusiasm that they would when a primary school teacher asks for a volunteer to take the class rabbit home for the holidays. A speaker of this kind will be given much more attention than the three cups of tea I get offered and there will always be an army of people offering to carry things back to their car for them. Watching this excitement affirms to me that to remain in the game without such celebrity status I have to be good – really good – at commanding the room. I have nothing but the quality of my last performance to carry me through to the next. Don't get me wrong, I'm not knocking the reaction people have to a gardening superstar; I'm sure I react in just the same way. It only smarts a bit when you are introduced as a stand-in for a big name who has pulled out at the last minute.

My satisfaction is knowing I have saved the day and the finances of clubs on many occasions!

I've lost count of how many talks I've done over the years, but it must be over a hundred now. Along the way I have had my share of disasters. I now no longer take a mobile into the building, after my uncle called me repeatedly during a talk and I failed to mute my phone. My phone has never entered a venue after that fateful day and remains firmly in the glove box of the car. If you can mute it, it's tempting to use your phone as a timer but I wouldn't advise it. Seeing a message pop up from a friend halfway through your description of how to combat aphid is bound to put you on the back foot. Halls usually have a clock, but if not I have often found myself borrowing a watch from a member of the audience. It's usually a rather over-sized gentleman's timepiece that is offered and I've discovered that wearing someone else's watch is a little creepy. Don't know why but it is. I must put a request in for a wristwatch of my own this Christmas.

One of the most memorable moments in all my years doing talks was accidentally speaker-bombing an archaeological club's event. I'd been searching for a hall in a remote village for what seemed like hours (admittedly, it was probably more like minutes) and at last I had spotted a hall fully lit up. I pulled into the car park and rushed through the door with my luggage.

'Evening all,' I said.

They all looked me up and down but no one said anything. It's not unusual to be met by silence when you arrive as a speaker. I started to unroll my extension lead. After a good few minutes, a bearded man in a cardigan asked, 'Who are you?'

'I'm your speaker for this evening.'

A look of panic came over his face and he explained that this was the archaeological society, and I must be in the wrong hall. How embarrassing – I can't believe they let me unpack and unwind before showing me the door.

I've experienced a power cut mid-way through my seasonal gardening tasks talk and the group were so keen to continue that they candlelit the hall (this was rather wonderful), I've been given the wrong date and driven several hours to be met by a distraught, tearful and rather apologetic speaker secretary and I've also had the chairperson of a group pass out whilst introducing me! (Painkillers for a bad hip coupled with a glass of wine at the start of the evening was the cause.) The worst thing that can happen to a speaker is to be booked on the evening of the club's Annual General Meeting. Unless, that is, like me you actually find the whole process entertaining and/or fascinating. At one memorable AGM I was asked to sit on the stage and wait until after the business of the meeting was over to start the talk. I was in full view of the audience. Having been brought up well, I patiently sat with a look of interest, accompanied with an occasional head nod where appropriate. Then the chairperson said, 'We have had all our good speakers for the year now and we are left with the cheaper speakers'. Sitting on the stage whilst this comment was floating around the room was absolutely crushing. I really had been put in the cheap seat in more ways than one. It ended up being the hardest talk I had ever given.

Your duties are usually not over when you've finished your talk. The most challenging part of any evening for me is judging the Garden on a Plate, Best Autumn Arrangement or the winning garden photograph. It's rather awkward studying the entries when you know the whole room is watching you. You can almost feel their eyes burning into your back. The problem always occurs when you pick 'the same old winner' – the person who always scoops up the club's first prize. You'll soon know if you've done this as you'll hear the sighs from all corners of the room when the winner's name is read out. Once you have announced the competition winners, it is often time to draw the winning raffle tickets. I'm always tempted to call them out in the style of a bingo caller, but I've refrained so far. In some cases the raffle prizes are clearly a mix of unwanted presents or previous unclaimed winnings. Dodgy wine, bath bombs, second-hand gardening books, talcum powder and bars of Imperial Leather soap seem to be familiar regulars of the raffle table. Why this brand of soap has so often been a feature I will never know – it's great for washing muddy hands, I suppose. Having grown up with a mother and grandmother who were members of the Women's Institute I have seen the panic that sets in ten minutes before a meeting as they searched the house for a prize. On more than one occasion I have tried to rescue the last packet of biscuits from being thrown into the mix. It's amazing how agile some older people can be when there is a prize to be picked from the table. They almost do the cha-cha-cha or tango as they pirouette to the front of the room.

Evenings are often rounded off with tea and cake. I'll never turn down a cup of tea. On occasion I have had three people skip over independently with tea and cake – refusing them would seem rather churlish. However, I am uncomfortably aware that three cups of tea might cause me an issue on the journey home – my bladder is good but not that good. Cake should never be refused as this would be seen as being insulting. I've started to take a Tupperware container with me so I can take treats home for the following day – also useful emergency rations if I am likely to get stuck in a snowdrift on the way home.

After a talk, I get a mini high. This is the feeling I love, and I should imagine it's why comedians enjoy the pressure of stand-up. The drive home is a good way to unwind. The journey to a talk is spent talking to myself and practicing how I will introduce myself but on the way home I'll tune into Radio 4 and listen to some scientific or arts programme that I don't have a hope in hell of understanding. Music stations are a no-go as I can't resist a good sing-along and by this point my voice is tired. The following day I am shattered but full of enthusiasm for my next voyage into the unknown.

The New Screen Scene

March 2020, and the UK is in lockdown – did it really happen? My memories of the early days of the Covid-19 pandemic feel like something I made up as part of a mad dream after eating too much cheese. The reality of the situation was unbelievably hard for so many, and I won't dwell on those painful times, but the one good thing to come out of it was that gardening suddenly became a priority for many, even those who had never considered it as a pastime before. Potting on, pricking out and planting offered us hope and, in many instances, an escape from those you were imprisoned in your house with. At last, gardening got the three cheers that it has long deserved. The nation was growing seeds in any available vessel: old tin cans, yoghurt pots, loo roll tubes and any other suitable container from the recycling bin. The *Blue Peter* generation were at last getting to put their make do and mend skills to the test – and were sharing their every move on social media. Gardening was trending – who'd have thought it? It seemed to me that people were at last catching on to what I had always known: gardening is the best medicine for mental and physical wellbeing. It's just a shame that it took a pandemic for people to find this out.

Being fortunate enough to live in the countryside, lockdown offered me a taste of what life might have been like for me if I had never had to work. There was time to experiment with making jam and elderflower cordial. I baked bread, grew hundreds of plants from seed, took up painting and sat in the garden listening to opera on the radio. I had become a medley of Nigella Lawson, Sarah Raven and Montserrat Caballé.

There was always a vase of freshly picked garden flowers on the table, something delicious in the kitchen and Joe Wicks doing a workout on the television. I would like to make it very clear here that I did not personally take part in any of Joe's fitness classes (this was my son's domain) – exercise was not my priority and during the lockdown my Lycra remained firmly in the drawer. Apart from the odd leisurely cycle up a country lane to admire the wildflowers, my focus was on floating around the garden at a wonderfully slow pace. My life has always been full throttle, and this was the first time I had experienced slow motion living. I loved it. I could've got used to this lifestyle and, as the weeks passed, I realised that much of my personality and passions are packed away so that they don't interfere with the daily grind. I'm convinced I'd be a far more interesting person if my bohemian lifestyle could be indulged. Time is the most precious commodity and I've never had enough of it.

The obvious downside to this serene existence was that I wasn't making any money. With many magazines tightening their belts, and as we were not able to open the garden to the public, I needed, like everyone else, to think outside the box. No one could gather together so the talks I regularly gave to gardening clubs were all scratched out of my diary – it was time to wake up and get busy.

Early in the pandemic I had come up with an idea to present a gardening talk via video link to supporters of a local hospice to raise funds for the charity. Tickets for this event sold well and, although the prospect of mastering the unknown world of online was terrifying, I was determined to dip my toe in the water. Post-pandemic, communicating with others online comes as second nature to most of us, but at the time it was like being part of a science fiction movie. If you'd told me ten years ago that it would be possible to talk to hundreds of people at once on your computer, I'd have told you that you needed an early night!

After my first success I was eager to give this new method of communicating a go, in the hope it would generate some income. I promoted myself as an online garden speaker and a few forward-thinking gardening clubs were brave enough to go for it.

It was essential for both myself and the speaker secretary to have a practice session before the real event. For most of the groups, I was to be their first experience of an online speaker. We would discuss how to use the functions and plan a disaster strategy. 'What if the internet is down?' 'What phone number should I call if you don't appear?' 'Is there a chance of a power cut?' Looking back, our concerns were trivial really, when you consider everything that was going on in the world. Everyone was edgy about the process and treated it as if we were organising a moon landing. This was new to us all. We were boldly going where no one else had before.

Talks would often be booked for the evenings. This is a tricky time in my household. Before each talk I would sternly warn my family that the use of the internet was strictly prohibited for the duration. Music, speaking and even moving too enthusiastically was also not permitted – they were to remain silent or leave the premises. Living in a very old house with creaky floorboards and thin walls, it's nearly impossible to shut out the activities of family life but I was determined that nothing would stop my train of thought or interfere with the Wi-Fi strength. The dog was even banished to the garden and a large sign would be placed outside the door, requesting that visitors or deliveries did not use the door knocker. Extreme, I know, but I had to get this right.

Before each talk I would set up my background. Vases of flowers and houseplants were propped up on books and I would appear as if I was emerging out of a jungle or flower border. My very long lockdown hair was tied up in a wartime headscarf or put into a bun. Make-up was applied and a bright top worn. The bottom part of my outfit was irrelevant. Glasses of water were at the ready and the lighting was spot on. I was being paid to do a good job and that's what I would do. There was no way of knowing how long we would be restricted and I was very aware that this could be my only income stream for weeks, months or perhaps even years.

As soon as I entered the meeting, my anxiety levels would drop. I had landed on the moon successfully. What a relief to see others, safely tucked up in their homes and what a joy to hear them chatting with their gardening friends. I hadn't realised it initially, being focused on my own concerns, but soon I saw that these virtual events were a lifeline to so many. They were a crucial way for those living on their own (or those that were sick of talking to the same partner for weeks) to have some form of human contact. Each online event came with its own magical moment –

not from me but from the audience. Watching the screen fill up with people and hearing the goings on in their homes was all the entertainment we needed. A screen full of the faces of strangers became a comfort and a joy.

The excitement starts from the moment the host lets people in. 'Can you see me?' 'I can hear you all but I can't see you?' 'I'd like to be in the cube next to Barbara – can someone move me?'

This is where established friendships play their part – fellow club members were always quick to offer IT advice and save the day. We mustn't forget that for some people, the pandemic was the first time they had been faced with a computer. Many didn't realise that we'd be able to see and hear the activities in their homes; some had tipped their camera to show the ceiling rather than simply turn their video off. A common sight was a younger member of the family setting up their older, or less IT literate, relative as the talk began. For some, it really was like being in control of a rocket. They were going live and entering the world of cyberspace.

I began to love those moments before a talk more and more. This was often the time that people took the chance to chat about family, the weather and their gardens. It offered golden material and I often found myself asking people how much their new grandchild weighed at birth or what Netflix series they were watching. We all need a chat and although the advice I was there to deliver was informative it was just as much about checking in on people.

During the height of the first wave of the pandemic, there was frequently news shared of the loss of a friend or mutual acquaintance due to Covid-19. The love and concern I witnessed was quite remarkable. These moving moments confirmed that gardening and other local clubs are so important in everyday life. They connect people and ensure that communities stay linked. As far as I'm concerned, their survival is vital. The organisers and I were right to give so much thought to the planning of these gatherings.

When you deliver a talk in person to a roomful of people you can only make assumptions about the type of home they live in, if you consider it at all. When they are seated in front of you in their houses, however, you gain an appreciation of the wide variety of people who share a love of gardening. Scanning through the little tiles of people on the screen is an insight. Some have been propped up in bed and obviously unwell, others are in headphones trying to block out a busy child-filled household carrying on behind them, and you'll see some in rather grand beamed sitting rooms and others in studies at desks piled high with paperwork and books. I might be welcoming them into my home, but they are also welcoming me. Any type of background is fine, but I'm afraid I do draw the line at people eating their tea. It can be quite off-putting if a member of your audience is trying to suck a long piece of spaghetti into their mouth as you explain the art of overwintering fuchsias! Tea, coffee or even a glass of wine or Prosecco I thoroughly approve of, however.

At the start of the pandemic, most hosts, including myself, hadn't mastered the art of mute all – the most essential command of the show. I was and still am amazed and amused by how many people insisted on regularly muting and unmuting themselves during a talk. I've had *The Archers* theme tune in the background, cats walking in front of the screen and flashing their bottoms at me (for some reason the cat owner often seems to think this is cute!) and on one occasion I heard a distance voice saying, 'How long is she going to talk for?' – apparently this was from an uninterested husband and not an official attendee, fortunately. On more than one occasion, there would be a reason for me to stop and say, 'Whoever is talking to their partner about their plans for the weekend, we can all hear you!'

Giving an online talk is the strangest thing and far more difficult than speaking in person at a venue. You are literally talking to yourself with no reaction. When a camera is turned off anything can be going on. You have no idea if they have muted you and gone to bed, switched on the TV or are loving every second – you're completely in the dark about whether you have hit the spot with your presentation. You must continue to smile through it all and keep your energy high for up to an hour. I compare it to being a children's TV presenter. Each expression needs to be exaggerated and your voice must offer different volumes and emotions to keep everyone engaged. It's hard to keep people interested in just one person's voice. The other thing that you must get used to is looking at yourself for an hour or more – another good reason for surrounding yourself with plants!

Once I mastered this new way of communicating, I was away. Without even putting fuel in the car, packing a bag or boarding a plane I have been able to give talks all over the UK and abroad, in Japan, Ireland and America among others. I've been welcomed into well over a thousand people's homes and all without taking my slippers off.

Launched from the Top Floor

We all have different ways of sorting things out in our heads and finding a release. Some go running, whereas others paint or swim. I write. As I run my fingers across a keyboard I feel as if I am dancing. Ever since I was a teenager, I have kept diaries and have always felt so much better for writing down my feelings and experiences. (I have my suspicions that my mother once found my college diaries, as on occasion she has reminded me never to write down anything so secret that you wouldn't want anyone else to read it, so I assume this was her way of suggesting that I destroy them!). Most of what I type is never intended to be seen by anyone else – and some is so private I often delete it afterwards for fear of it being discovered (proof that I do listen to my mother on occasion).

As part of this feel-good therapy, a few years ago I started to keep a diary of what was going on in the garden day-to-day purely as a record for myself. It was to be a personal reminder of the weather, the activity and the days: which were busy or not with visitors, what was particularly beautiful in flower, any interesting events or challenges I'd faced. I had never intended for it to be for public consumption.

However, after casually mentioning my little diary in a business meeting, before I knew what was happening I had a deadline to complete it and the excitement of turning it into a book. A local independent press was excited by the idea and convinced me to share their enthusiasm. If I'd planned it, I suspect it wouldn't have happened but thanks to a twist of fate I was about to become an author. I like to think of my book as being self-sown and not purposefully propagated – a chance seedling that took root.

When I think of authors, I picture them as sophisticated people who craft their words longhand on paper at a desk in a study that is covered in books from floor to ceiling. I know this isn't the reality at all, but still, it's how I choose to view them in my mind's eye. They aren't at all like me, doing my writing on a dirt-engrained potting bench whilst drinking tea poured from a flask and welcoming customers through the gates of the open garden. However much I'd like to, I cannot shut out the world and dedicate myself to writing undisturbed. My first book, *Diary of a Modern Country Gardener*, had to fit into my chaotic life. If I wasn't writing from the potting bench, I was completing a chapter at the kitchen table whilst waiting for the potatoes to boil or assisting with homework. It wasn't unusual for my son to be kicking his indoor football over my head or testing out his keepy-up skills to the backing track of ABBA whilst I attempted to write. On many occasions I got up from the table and demanded silence. Of course, this fell on deaf ears and life in our household continued as normal. I even tried reading sections from the book to the family, but I would look up after a few paragraphs to find that they had left the room (On the plus side, I have now learnt the quickest way to get the room to myself is not an appeal for silence but threatening to read a chapter aloud!). In an ideal world, I would have retreated to a remote log cabin, placed a desk in front of a window with an amazing view and written for hours on end without disturbance. This, however, was never going to be possible. In a strange way, I hold this book dearer because it was created alongside the everyday goings-on of my life as a mother and a gardener. It has reality running right through it.

I was fortunate enough to be involved in every stage of creating my book – everything from finding a talented illustrator to taking the photographs myself as the garden evolved. For a book to have a heart, I believe you need that close involvement and complete connection with it. The downside of immersing yourself to such an extent and giving your soul to a project is that you are in danger of being broken if it isn't received well. Do not underestimate the fear that an author goes through in the weeks leading up to publication. How will it be reviewed? Will it sell? It is *terrifying*. Sleepless nights come with the territory. Very few people will be aware of the inner turmoil that you are facing as the on-sale date approaches. Publishing a book is quite possibly one of the bravest things I have done. After having written so many magazine articles in my career you'd have thought I'd be cool as a cucumber about it, but it just doesn't compare. My mother insisted on keeping every magazine I had ever written for and storing them in her loft until I told her to stop a few years ago. I was in fear that my back catalogue would eventually fall through the ceiling. My book was first published in hardback, so I'm hoping that she hasn't started stockpiling those instead as I fear this would put her in certain danger!

Before the reviews comes the launch. Your book might mean everything to you but until people have a physical copy in their hands it's hard to drum up enthusiasm from anyone other than your publisher. A few people had read an advance copy and said kind words but the launch party was my first real indication of whether anyone was interested at all. On 20th February 2020 at 6.30pm guests would be arriving at the iconic Hatchard's bookshop on London's Piccadilly. Or would they? My publisher and editor had a plan to lure people in by offering Herefordshire gin cocktails and a glitzy location that would tempt reluctant travellers. This world-famous bookshop, which claims to be the oldest in the UK, was the place where, in 1804, the meeting about founding what is now the Royal Horticultural Society was held. It seemed the perfect place for a gardening book to be launched.

Knowing now what was soon to come in 2020, with the Covid-19 pandemic and national lockdown, I feel blessed to have had my launch just in time. But in the days leading up to it I did not feel so lucky. The weather was not on my side. Storms hit the country to such an extent that I headed to London a day early – there was no way on earth I'd miss my own party! My husband was bemused by my enthusiasm to travel prematurely, so I left him behind. For once I was proved right, as trains were cancelled and he had to make an arduous journey the following day partly by bus, which involved a detour from Herefordshire into Wales. This was the one time I was happy to say, 'I told you so'. We had a romantic reunion at Paddington station. He had dramatically battled through the elements to reach me just in time.

The walk to the bookshop from the hotel will be etched in my memory forever. My husband and son are remarkably laid back whereas I am like a wound-up spring when I have an event to go to. I'm convinced they walked far slower than ever before and stopped to look at every shop window. Under my instruction I had told them to wear smart shoes and on no account trainers. I regretted this deeply as the lack of bounce in their feet slowed them to a snail's pace. They even dared to break the walk and get a coffee. Were they serious? Had they no concept of the stress I was under? I rushed ahead of them like a woman possessed. In fact, I was behaving like a pheasant trying to cross a road – moving erratically with an air of panic. As I darted down the pavement, I would occasionally catch a glance of my reflection in a shop window. In hindsight, my outfit wasn't great. Not only had I gone dressed in a suit with palm leaves all over it (an outfit that makes me look like a tree in a primary school production of *The Jungle Book*), but I also now had a look of fear on my face that wouldn't shift. No amount of makeup could resolve it. Add to this the fact that I was carrying a cocktail shaker that I'd bought to help mix the gin and the picture of this unconventional 'author' was complete – I had turned myself into a cartoon character. I had visions of just a couple of loyal friends or relatives turning up. I was determined that this wasn't going to be a book that only my family bought. Would I be standing by myself with a rictus grin, a huge stack of books and a large bottle of gin in this fabulous literary palace where movie stars and world-famous authors had launched bestsellers? A book launch with low footfall and little sparkle isn't how you want to kick off your journey as an author.

As I approached the bookshop alone, I couldn't believe what I could see. On a giant easel was an impressive gold-framed poster displaying the words 'An Evening with Tamsin Westhorpe'. My family might have been a million paces behind me, and the London streets paved in puddles rather than gold, but I was elated. This gardener without an A level to her name had that name in a frame on Piccadilly. Suddenly I felt calmer – I'd made it on time, in one piece, and my fear turned to excitement.

If you've never been to Hatchard's, you must visit. It's magical – the sort of establishment where you might buy a wand rather than a book. This is the type of building that I imagine comes alive at night once everyone has gone home. There is so much history here and it oozes such charm that it simply must be wonderfully haunted by authors of the past. To have a book of mine being cradled by its ancient shelves was an honour. Bestselling authors such as Salman Rushdie and Enid Blyton have walked through those doors (although I suspect they weren't dressed as a tree). Baroness Margaret Thatcher was another famous visitor, and when Bette Davis arrived to sign her book, the crowds of fans who descended closed Piccadilly to traffic. I wasn't expecting quite the same footfall but a girl can dream.

I was being 'launched' from the top floor and, as I stood at the top of the impressive staircase that runs up through the middle of the shop like a spine, I had the perfect view. This is the moment that you really know who your friends are as, let's face it, a book launch on a very wet evening in central London in late-winter isn't a small ask. Standing at the top of the stairs, leaning over the balcony, reminded me of being a child when my parents would have people over for dinner parties. My sisters and I would be sent to bed but would spend the evening at the top of the stairs, listening to the adults' conversations. In this case I *was* the conversation, so I needed to get involved and not just be an onlooker in pyjamas.

Soon the guests began to arrive. Up those famous bookshop stairs came friends, family, past colleagues, new colleagues and all sorts of people I admire greatly. When I heard the voice of the late Peter Seabrook, my evening was complete. Imagine having the gardener that you had avidly watched on television as a child attend your book launch decades later. It may sound corny, but seeing such wonderful people climbing up towards me I wanted to sing 'Top of the World' – there's a Carpenter's song for every occasion, you know!

My plan for the evening was to take tips from Bridget Jones. I was going to 'circulate oozing intelligence and fool myself into thinking that I was the intellectual equal of everyone else in the room'. After a few moments of trying this, I quickly realised, as Bridget did, that it's impossible to be someone you're not. A gin cocktail later and I was back to being me (or at least a slightly tipsy version). I bounced around the room, trying to speak to everyone although, as I still had shades of flighty pheasant about me, I'm sure I failed to have a decent conversation with anyone.

After the mingling, and speeches, came the book signing part of the evening. Well, this is an odd thing to do. I had invested in a rather good pen, which I quickly realised was a complete liability. Good pens never dry fast enough, and I ended up with lots of signed books airing out on the desk, lined up like knickers on an Aga. When under pressure, I also lost any ability to spell. When someone asked me to sign a book to Joan or Marie or an equally easy to spell name, I went blank. So, yes, I was the author who asked everyone to slowly spell out their name for me – by this point, I suspect they were very worried about having committed to buying the book.

I left that evening feeling wonderful. I can honestly say that I have never felt so overwhelmed that so many people bothered to make the effort to join me for my book launch. They probably have no idea how much it meant. The whole experience of writing that first book was more than I ever dreamt of and ending such a solitary occupation with a party was the perfect end to one part of it and the beginning of another once the book was in the world. So if you are ever asked to go to a book launch – however much you might not fancy it on the night – please go. Every author needs support and will be eternally thankful for it. That Hatchard's poster in a gold frame is now hanging in my study and, if I ever feel unloved, I take one look at it and I'm all good.

Back Garden Antics

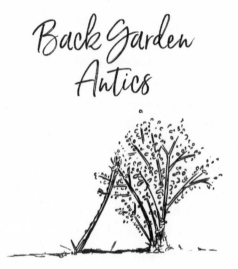

With such a busy season at work, I had neglected my own garden. I live in a very old and quirky house that was once one farmhouse but has long since been split into two. Many moons ago the garden was a farmyard, so underneath the lawn are the foundations of old outbuildings and in places, now grassed over, you'll come across the cobbles of the yard. When I hit these stony skeletons of the past with my spade, I am reminded of the history of the place.

The plot is long rather than wide and at the end there is an amazing view of the surrounding countryside. The garden's main focal point is the shed – it sits right at the end of the plot and slap-bang in the middle so your eye is inexorably drawn to it. Why the previous owner felt it necessary to place it there, where it is both impractically far from everything and an eyesore, I will never know, but I've accepted it's unlikely we'll ever have the energy to move it. This garden is always far from a show piece, but on this particular late-summer morning it was looking a little more than usually rough around the edges and crying out for my attention.

So, on a warm September day and one of my rare days off, I had decided to give my back garden some much overdue care. I marched up the garden to the shed to get the ladder out. My family were out so I had the place to myself and wouldn't be sidetracked by requests to stand in goal as I had been all summer. Extracting something from this distant shed is no mean feat as my husband is Mr Security. There are more security measures in place for the shed than the house!

Three padlocks later I'd at last gained entry – looking around me I wondered which item he was so frightened of being stolen. Could it be the old kids' bikes with very few spokes on the wheels? Or perhaps the badminton net so knotted and holey it looks like it has been used to catch a shark? I had no time to stop and ponder.

Today, I was going to break the back of the gardening jobs and make my mark on the plot. Apart from taking a short break at lunchtime to give an online lecture to a garden club I had dedicated the day to long overdue practical tasks. The beauty of presenting through a computer screen is that you can quickly change your top to give your talk without anyone knowing that you have wet knees and grass stains on your trousers.

My enthusiasm for the day's activities was high and I was on a one-woman mission. I'd purposely left my mobile phone in the house as nothing was going to disturb me. September is a busy and rather beautiful time in the garden. Although autumn is around the corner it can offer the most wonderful summer weather and the flowers associated with this month are often striking. There's plenty of tasks on the list, with deadheading, seed harvesting and mowing at the top, but I'd decided to prioritise pruning.

In our garden we have a row of five aronia (chokeberry) trees that have each been grafted onto a sorbus rootstock. I know they are grafted as the sorbus annoyingly throws up shoots from the bottom of each tree with impressive vigour. These trees cope well with our very waterlogged garden in winter and equally well in the hard baked clay of summer. They have also remained remarkably unscathed after being pelted with footballs time and time again by my son. Aronia berries are said to be very good for you, but I have yet to discover a way to consume them – so far, my experience has been a bitter one, quite literally, but the birds seem to appreciate the autumn feast. With their far from appealing taste no wonder they carry the nickname of 'chokeberry'!

Helping to run an open garden, I always feel as if my work is on show – I think this is a common experience, and we 'show gardeners' tend to kick back and relax when it comes to our own plots. I enjoy pottering with my plants in my front garden, but the back is used more as a place for family fun. We are fortunate to be surrounded by fields on two sides, so the only prying eyes tend to be those of the sheep that graze over the hedge. The purpose of buying this house was for our son to have a place that he could build a relationship with nature in. There are no rules and no out-of-bound areas. We have patches that have been left to naturalise where nettles thrive. In amongst these nettles are some rather less natural punctured footballs, and the odd cricket ball that my son always claims he can't find. At either end are homemade football goals and the lawn is grazed with marks from striker's celebrations (not mine I hasten to add, as I'm more likely to be the goalie who let the ball in.)

As well as being security-minded, my husband is a great one for collecting up and using old pallets and as a result of this strange habit he has made a rather impressive garden sofa out of scrap wood. This generously sized country garden has given us and our visiting friends so much pleasure over the years. It's been the venue for bonfire night celebrations, camping parties, Easter egg hunts and mini sports days. I recall a little boy coming to play with my son when they were both at primary school. I had decided that it would be fun to give the boys fish fingers and chips wrapped in newspaper for tea and suggested that they ate in the garden den. When the boy was collected by his mother, he quickly told her that we were so poor we didn't even own any plates! I'm sure that little chap has never forgotten the adventure of visiting our garden.

But I digress. My first task that day was the aronia trees. My intention is to keep them neat and to a manageable size, so the new growth needed a trim. To do this I leapt up the ladder to give the chokeberries their annual haircut and remove the whippy stems. As I worked, I reflected on how lucky I was to be fit (truly this is what I was thinking about). I'd visited a garden the evening before to offer advice to its owner on how to make her large borders more manageable, having sadly lost her beloved husband who was a keen gardener, so this subject was on my mind. It wasn't a remarkable topic for me to be pondering (although somewhat ironic, as I was imminently about to discover), as I can't tell you how often I am asked how to make a garden easier to manage. The harsh reality of life is that our physical strength can't be relied on indefinitely – we have yet to discover the potion that will give us eternal youth and fitness (maybe the super healthy fruits of the aronia hold the answer?). Gardening is a physical hobby, which is great as it keeps us fit but also means that when age does catch up with us it cannot be ignored. Ultimately, gardens must change so that we can keep them easily and feel relaxed about them. Leaving your much-loved home because you can no longer mow the lawn yourself or cut the hedges can be devastating, and a little forethought can mean the difference between keeping things manageable and everything getting out of control. Although mowing can be a challenge for some, I am never one to encourage the lifting of a lawn. Time and time again I hear of people replacing their turf with a large sheet of plastic or old carpet that is to be covered in gravel in the pursuit of that holy grail, 'low maintenance'. I can promise you that your delight in its initial appearance will be short-lived and in no time at all weeds will return and the local cats will make it their litter tray. It's far easier to find a teenager who will mow your lawn for a few quid than it is to find someone patient enough to hand-weed a sea of somewhat whiffy gravel.

Back to the job in hand! My pruning was going well. The sun was shining, the sky was blue and my secateurs were sharp. But everything was about to change with one fateful move. I leant in to prune a central branch and the ladder went from under me. For a moment I thought I would remain animated in mid-air, but of course I did not. The brutal reality was that I was lying flat on my back. This wasn't good and I knew it – pain and shock had taken over my body. A series of expletives came pouring out of my mouth. F**k, s**t and many, many more. As I am not one for confrontation (in fact I'll run a mile to avoid it) swearing has always been the way I release my anger – I'm not proud of it but it works. Not many people expect a gardener who tends pretty flowers to have such a foul mouth!

As I lay on the lawn surrounded by prunings, and once I had stopped swearing, I did a mini assessment of the damage. Had I broken my ribs, punctured a lung or just winded myself? I had landed on my back, but the pain in my chest was the prominent issue. I couldn't sit up but could move my fingers and toes. I knew that trying to move wasn't advisable, so I decided that the best cause of action was to shout and scream for help. Our neighbours' houses are fairly distant and none of them have windows that look over our property, so I knew it was pretty unlikely I'd be able to raise them, but I was going to give it my best shot to attract attention. Did anyone come? Did they f**k! (Mind you, if my neighbours had heard me they would've had a job to get to the scene. Mr Security padlocks the side gate to the garden and my neighbours are of an age where attempting to climb over might have resulted in another casualty).

I don't think I have shouted so loud and so long ever before in my life and to be ignored was devastating. My chest felt as if it had a tight metal band around it and breathing was getting harder and harder. I'm not sure how long I shouted for before getting up, but it must've been a good 10 minutes. Having done a first aid course a few years prior to this I knew I wasn't meant to move but human instinct takes over. I had to get to the house to raise the alarm. To get to my feet I rolled onto my side and used my arms to push myself up. Moving was agony and getting up a slow process but I was determined as the alternative was to remain on the lawn for possibly hours.

As I struggled to my feet, thoughts of the open garden I run with my uncle ran through my mind like an encyclopaedia of gardening on fast forward. Who would lift the dahlias? How would

I help plant the tulips? And then I had something else to worry about too. Is it wrong that my first thoughts are of the garden rather than my health? Am I so obsessed with my passion for plants that I've lost a grip on all other aspects of my life?

Somehow, I managed to hobble to the house. I must have looked like something out of a zombie movie as I dragged myself down the 1-acre garden. I know how lucky we are to have a large garden but on this occasion I wished it was far smaller.

Having made it inside the house I grabbed the phone then my blue diary. You might think you don't need a diary to call 999 and you'd be right, but for some reason my first thought was to contact the speaker secretary of the group I was presenting a talk to later that day. Phone reception in rural Herefordshire is dreadful but moving to the hot spot in the house was not an option as I was in crippling pain. After many attempts, that magical mobile reception bar came up on my phone and it started to dial. I felt for the poor woman at the end of the line who answered and received only the words 'I've had an accident just now so won't be speaking today – I need to ring an ambulance – goodbye'. Now if that doesn't make them remember me as a speaker then I'm not sure what will (in fact, they have since rather generously rebooked me, and on that day I will ensure that I wrap myself in cotton wool).

You'll be relieved to hear that my next call was to the emergency services – as you can see my priorities are rather skewed. When my husband arrived home to find me on the sofa reeling in pain his words were, 'What have you done now?' I wasn't aware that I was that much of a liability, but I suppose I must be. I'll admit that I do have a habit of looking at a physical task and assuming that I can do it easily. My eyes are bigger than my biceps and after 20 years of marriage he knows this only too well! He has often had to finish off a task I have abandoned such as trying to cut through a large branch with a mini hand saw. After taking a longer look at me he hastily packed me an overnight bag – his enthusiasm and efficiency was slightly unnerving and suggested that he didn't want to be in sole charge of the woman shouting instructions at him from the sofa. He'd accurately identified that this time curing my mess would mean I'd need more than a cup of tea and an afternoon in front of the TV.

We then both decided that it would be wise to remove my trousers. For some reason, we felt it would make life easier for the ambulance crew – I suspect we were just panicking at this point. As he helped me to carefully wiggle out of my trousers, I noticed something. 'I've got a wet leg,' I said in a pathetic voice, to which he replied, 'It's blood. I think you've impaled yourself with a stick.' His face now revealed a slightly more panicked look – but not for me. We have a cream sofa: this was going to be a devil to clear up! It was then that I realised I was wearing my smallest pants and odd socks. They were not just any old odd socks but one Christmas sock and one plain grey. Why, in God's name? It was only September and I have hundreds of matching socks at my disposal. It was also the moment that the stark reality of my hairy legs hit me. Add to this the fact that my husband, trying his best to solve a problem, had helped to dress me in a pair of his enormous football shorts and the picture of a gardening lunatic was complete. Of course, someone this crazy-looking would stand on the top step of an ancient ladder and fall off it.

The ambulance angels (as I like to call them) arrived quickly. Our house is a very old building and doesn't have such mod cons as central room lights. We have a couple of lamps with low wattage bulbs in the sitting room so it's fairly dark (the great advantage to this is that you can't see the cobwebs). 'Can you put the lights on?' asked the paramedic. To which my husband and I replied in unison: 'They *are* on.' To throw more light onto the situation, my husband rushed to get his most powerful torch and shone it directly at me. There is nothing worse than being under a spotlight when you look and feel so bad, but needs must.

The overnight bag that was packed with such enthusiasm earlier was going to be required after all. It was a visit to the hospital for me. As I lay in the ambulance, looking down at my holly-adorned Christmas sock, thoughts of the garden continued to swirl around my head. To take my mind off my concerns I started to talk to the paramedic about all and sundry – I'm sure this, the socks and my shorts added to her sense of concern for the mental state of her patient. She asked me on one too many occasions if I had hit my head!

Upon arrival I was placed in the trauma unit. The immediate trauma for me was needing a wee. Did I really have to experience my first bed pan? Alas, I did. As I sat on my impressively robust cardboard throne the reality of the situation started to sink in. I'm not quite sure what was the most distressing – being in pain myself or seeing other people's pain. I'm not good with blood so every time a patient entered the ward, I closed my eyes. The last thing the nurses needed was a fainter.

After a few hours of all the normal check-ups I was wheeled through the hospital for a scan. Again, as I was pushed through the corridors, my view was those bloody odd socks. Further embarrassment was to come when I realised the bra I was wearing was, quite simply, horrid. I might be a gardener who by profession spends her life in muddy trousers and past-their-best tops, and whose only previous requirement of undergarments was to keep me warm but my view was rapidly changing. Never before have I felt such a strong desire to invest in frilly and fancy lingerie but after this I was going all out. I've always used the excuse that I'm just gardening so it didn't matter – but oh boy, how wrong I was. Underwear is fundamental.

Time is a strange thing when you are in pain. It passes unnoticed and you lose track of it. My results from the scan were the next hurdle for me to jump. 'Well, young lady, you have been very lucky,' said the doctor. Although he was wearing a mask, I could see that he had the kindest eyes. For a moment I thought I'd got away with it and would be back in the border in a flash. However, his next words as he held my hand were: 'You have broken your spine.'

These are words that no one should ever have to hear. The ongoing Covid-19 pandemic had meant that I was at hospital on my own – no friends or family were allowed to accompany me. To be honest, I'd preferred it until that point. The pressure of having worried, bored and hungry relatives pacing up and down in the waiting room is a stress you don't need. I'd rather they were at home looking after my dog. This view of being alone quickly changed after receiving my diagnosis. The lack of support hit me and I suddenly realised how dependent I would be on the kindness of others. I was lucky to have a family waiting at home to leap into action, but many people aren't as fortunate. Imagine having an accident like this or worse and being completely alone.

Although the words were shocking, in fact my prognosis was positive. My fracture was stable, I could walk and all being well I would be fully recovered in twelve weeks. My biggest and most immediate challenge was informing my unaware mother, uncle and sisters of the news without sending them into shock. This caused me more pain and concern than any of my injuries. The person who loves to jump up and take action had had the rug pulled from under her. I was going to be incarcerated. Disaster for the dahlias, the dog and the almost non-existent dusting regime! I also had to face the embarrassment of people discovering that a garden writer who spends much of her life telling people how to garden safely had broken the rules. I should've known better than to go up a ladder without someone footing it. Yes, I had been a very silly girl and was now paying the price.

I spent just one night in hospital – one night was enough for me. Being placed on a ward with people who had been in hospital for some time meant that they were rather excited to have new company. With visitors restricted or non-existent, my fellow patients were eager for conversation. I, on the other hand – and this was very out of character – was not in the mood to talk. After eating a disappointing jacket potato the size of a testicle, I lay and looked at the ceiling. I was cross – not with the size of my hospital meal but with myself for being such an idiot.

The next time I was to smile was when I was collected by my husband the following day. The front passenger seat of the car was covered with a large black bin bag, slit open and spread out. At first I assumed my husband was concerned that I might wet myself as we travelled but as I easily slipped into the seat thanks to its plastic covering he congratulated himself on this very simple, very cheap mobility aid (and I congratulated myself on not being incontinent!).

Once home, my recovery time ticked by with the company of my friends: Netflix, painkillers, tea and cake. My ever-practical mother was quick to remind me that eating such large quantities of cake whilst you can't exercise is probably unwise – she was right, of course. I was forbidden from lifting anything and advised to keep moving very gently. I dreaded the long and agonising process of trying to sit up in my bed every morning and was just as keen to avoid getting into bed at night. Having a physical job, I am used to being exhausted when I hit the pillow, not struggling to sleep with pain.

After a few weeks, deadheading was about the only gardening task I could do without risk. Being in constant discomfort is exhausting and so was the guilt of not being able to help out at my uncle's open garden. I was useless and had to accept the fact that rushing or risking my recovery would only be detrimental. Closing my eyes to everything I should be doing was the only way forward.

This accident has changed the way I look at gardening. I now have first-hand experience of the frustration of not being able to look after my own patch and enormous empathy for those who see their once neatly tended plot start to deteriorate. Not having the physical ability to garden is hideous. I will revisit my research on how to make a garden easier and look at ways to avoid lifting – my previous advice focused on general energy saving but now I realise that every garden and gardener needs a unique diagnosis.

However, having said all that, the joy of being in a garden whilst feeling unwell is immeasurable. I spent many hours lying on the outside pallet sofa – it was by far the most comfortable place to be. On occasion, I did feel as if I was flat-packed and might be picked up by a forklift and transported somewhere at a moment's notice! Lying out in the garden with a soft breeze floating over you is the most healing thing in the world. You almost feel like you are being washed by the air – this was my version of forest bathing. I've always known how important being outside is for everyone but now I have hard evidence. There is so much to see that you can never be bored. Butterflies, bees and even a squirrel have approached my pallet chaise longue and birdsong is far more enjoyable than the sound of daytime TV.

So, now I am fully recovered, and with no lasting ill effects apart from wounded pride, what have I learnt from this episode? The first thing is that I must invest in a proper tripod gardening ladder designed for uneven ground. The one that I fell from was 20 years old and, in hindsight, not suitable for gardening. I will never climb a ladder again without someone footing it. When I'm home alone I'll stick to weeding. I've also learnt that gardening with your phone in your pocket is a sensible plan – but put it on silent mode, so you're not disturbed. Not being able to get out and about or physically work in the garden also confirmed to me exactly what I love doing. Here's my list of favourite things (with apologies to Julie Andrews):

Raindrops on roses…. And garden visiting, gardening, being outside, attending RHS Chelsea and watering my plants. I hated not being able to water my pots during my long convalescence. It's a task that those not interested in gardening often fail at miserably. Watering well once a day gives you time to admire your potted displays. Lastly, I like to be able to strip off knowing that my underwear is up to scratch. The Christmas socks are in the bin and the ancient ladder has been smashed up by my husband with his fencing mallet! I, on the other hand, am now back gardening but with two feet firmly on the ground.

Under Canvas Heist

ttending local country shows as a child, with classes for the funniest shaped vegetable and garden on a plate, were my very first experience of attending anything that resembled a gardening show. The best tasting strawberry jam or the biggest marrow were hotly contested prizes. I clearly recall my grandmother plating up her Victoria sponge for the judges. These idyllic and yet highly competitive events were the only experience I had of growing and showing throughout my childhood and teens. So when the opportunity arose to attend and exhibit at RHS Chelsea Flower Show in 1993 with my fellow students, I was beyond giddy and to say I was completely naive as to the scale of the event and its importance would be an understatement. Just to put into perspective how long ago this was, 1993 was the year that Ford launched the Mondeo, *Sleepless in Seattle* was in the cinema and Meatloaf was claiming 'I'd Do Anything For Love (But I Won't Do That)' – a sentiment that resonated hard with me at the time!

We were to create a scene with woodland and aquatic plants in the Great Marquee at Chelsea under the close supervision of our lecturer. This canvas construction, that reminded me of an enormous Girl Guides tent on steroids as soon as I entered it, was simply spectacular. If you have ever had the misfortune of camping in such a tent (obviously on a much smaller scale), you'll recall lying on the ground and being able to look out at the view through the gap at the bottom of the canvas as you snuggled down into your damp sleeping bag. Being kept awake by the creaking of the poles and the giggles of your fellow Girl Guides was all part of the adventure – it was like being Robinson Crusoe drifting out to sea on a raft with little protection from the elements. (I didn't last long as a Girl Guide, after loading the embers of the campfire into a black bag and placing them in the leader's car boot whilst they were still hot! I thought I was being helpful.) Yet despite my association with ill-fated camping trips, stepping inside Chelsea's giant marquee as a young woman is something I will never forget. The scale of endeavour of the exhibits, the precision and the sheer beauty of the plants was beyond anything I'd thought achievable. It was at this moment that I realised horticulture wasn't just a career path, it was the stuff of making dreams come true. Why had so many well-meaning adults turned their noses up at my request to be a gardener? Had they not seen the potential? I had stepped into the Hollywood of Horticulture.

Unless my memory mistakes me, we had to create our exhibit around one of the Great Marquee's mighty poles. I can't recall how long it took us to put up the exhibit, but I do remember using small snips and paintbrushes to perfect our display. The light in the marquee was very yellow – dreadful for plants and photography and seven years later, in 2000, the enormous marquee was replaced by a far more practical pavilion that is large enough to house 500

London buses. Although this updated model is far superior, I still hold a candle for the creaky old marquee that groaned every time the wind blew. I'd like to step back in time and experience that giant tent once more. One of my biggest regrets is that I didn't manage to buy one of the many canvas bags that the Great Marquee was made into after its time was over – I would have loved a memento of one of the most exciting experiences of my life.

In love with the whole idea of Chelsea, I was quick to offer to take our exhibit down when the show was over – any excuse to return to this sacred ground. Not long after the crowds had left on the last day, a stream of lorries and vans began to flood in. The drivers had been patiently waiting in Battersea Park for the green light to join the queue onto the showground. We took it in turns to wait outside the marquee and look out for our getaway vehicle. With no mobile phones back then, it was vital that we all listened to instruction. Eventually our van arrived and in now faded light we were tasked with quickly and efficiently loading up the vehicle as a matter of urgency. It was as if we were involved in a heist – communicating with our driver and creating a human chain to get plants to the vehicle as quickly as possible. There were people waiting behind us in their vehicles to reach their exhibits – very tired people at that. The last thing they wanted to see after weeks of preparing and showing were a bunch of students larking about.

Once on the road, our next stop was a service station on the motorway for a cuppa at about two in the morning. At every table there were nursery people enjoying a well earnt pit stop on their way home, going over the events of the show as they chatted. I could've sat there for hours earwigging. I was hooked but at the time, I assumed that this adventure in horticultural Hollywood would be a one off.

How wrong I was. The next time I was to return to RHS Chelsea as a professional was as a writer on press day. I wouldn't be wearing high vis or heavy steel toe-capped boots this time, but my smartest Sunday best. Who'd have thought it? The mere fact that I'd manged to get to London on my own was enough; to actually be entering the gates of RHS Chelsea Flower Show as part of my work was something else. (As an aside, it always strikes me as very strange that my career in horticulture leads me to travel to London on numerous occasions. It might be a city, but it is certainly a hub of horticultural activity – so much so that I wished my lecturers had given us a crash course in using the tube network. To this day I am like a mole lost in the network of tunnels).

Since my first press visit, this gardener's paradise has given me so much – including hay fever and blisters! Never attend this event without comfy shoes and an antihistamine. As soon as you step through the gates, you forget about the fact you are in a bustling city. It's like being in a bubble and nothing outside of it seems to matter whilst you are there. If my phone rings when I'm on the showground I'm unlikely to answer – I'm in the zone. I always go armed with every possible form of ID. The thought of not being able to enter due to lack of information to collect my pass fills me with fear. My passport and driving license are always in my pocket. In the old days, you were given a wristband as you entered that could only be cut off. I'd keep it on my arm for days – I wanted people to ask me what it was for. 'I've been to Chelsea, don't you know!'. I knew most people of my age would be far happier with a wristband for Glastonbury – but not me. I'll take the Great Marquee over a pop-up tent in the mud any day.

After attending for decades, you'd have thought that the sparkle would fade, but it most certainly hasn't. This is the one event in the year that I feel bereft if I miss it. As a writer and editor I would attend with the mission of turning over every stone to find a great story (not literally or I'd have been marched off site). It was my job to scope out the trends, the new plants, the charity links and the people stories. Digging deep into the reasoning behind each exhibit gives you even more cause to fall deeply in love with the whole event. It is on press day that my floral outfits get their outing. Bright, bold and blooming outrageous attire is welcomed here; I think the world would be a far better place if we all dressed like this every day. Interviewing designers and plantspeople about their gardens or exhibits, I have witnessed the sheer dedication of all the people involved. Months and months are put into the creation of this event and the emotional rollercoaster that the exhibitors go on involves fear, exhilaration and relief.

To experience an even stronger bond with Chelsea seemed impossible, but then, a few years ago, I was invited to be an RHS Gardens Judge. This must be one of my proudest achievements in life. The thought that the girl who once pushed the hostess trolley full of watering cans through offices was now being embraced by the judging team was just beyond my wildest dreams. To be asked to judge gardens created by some of the finest designers and landscapers in the world is something I never imagined I would be doing when I was litter-picking in the parks. That moment when the rope is dropped to allow you to step onto a show garden at Chelsea is incomparable to anything else. You are walking where few get a chance to tread.

This year I volunteered to help plant a garden at the event for a few days. Not knowing what the weather would bring, I had packed for every eventuality, as usual. Armed with secateurs, trowel, kneepads, my trusty flask and wearing my weighty steel toe-capped boots I headed through the famous gates with an army of other volunteers. Watching the event grow up around me and being in the heart of the action again confirmed that feeling from long ago, that what is created here is quite simply unbelievable. The calm and tranquillity that we see on the impressive TV coverage is a million miles from the organised chaos that comes before it. I was only a tiny part of the creative chaos this year and after three days of planting in the famous Chelsea soil I had to head home, back to my real world. I left for my train with no time to wash my hands or face. To be honest, I looked like I had been rolling in soil for days and landed in my seat exhausted. I was so tired that I had not realised that I was still wearing my knee pads, which had now slipped down to my calves, and my secateur holster was still fastened around the waistband of my dirty camouflage trousers. On arrival at my destination, a rather gorgeous and very smartly dressed man offered to help me with my bags. Did he take a fancy to my action woman attire or was he concerned for the state of exhaustion and dishevelment I was in? I will never know! The one thing I do know is that I would do it all over again, just for a slice of that Chelsea magic.

Whatever Next?

Recently someone called me a 'veteran of the gardening world'. Should I be annoyed or flattered? I suppose this is inevitable as I have now started to wear comfy shoes and put my glasses on a chain (both things I associate with people of a certain age). Note to fellow gardeners here – having your glasses on a chain really isn't sensible whilst working outside. I have been hooked to so many plants in recent weeks. It's like being a fly that constantly gets trapped in spiders' webs.

Having recently and reluctantly turned fifty, I've at last decided that it isn't all that bad. I was gifted so many bottles of Prosecco by friends that it is quite possible I will remain tipsy for the next decade. The other good news is that I share my momentous birthday year with a few of the world's most beautiful people. Jude Law, Gwyneth Paltrow and Cameron Diaz were also born in 1972 and they surely go to prove the point that fifty is the new forty. On entering this new decade, I asked myself whether I am now not so appealing as a writer or gardener, or am I at last deemed to be of an age where I have amassed enough knowledge to be called an expert? Only time will tell. Actually, the term expert slightly worries me – what is the marker that makes someone in their chosen field fit the category? Should one ever confess to being an expert? Are you simply setting yourself up for a fall? It is impossible to know everything about gardening so to be a true expert you need to live four times over or have dedicated many years to one particular plant group or growing technique. Being a flighty Gemini and always looking over my shoulder at the next thing, this type of dedication isn't something I could commit to.

The great thing about this hobby and career is that there's definitely more ways than one to do it. This is one reason why horticulture has held my attention for so long. Some might prick out their seedlings with a pencil whilst others would use a table fork. That's the beauty of growing plants. It's never dull and there's always plenty of experimenting and trial and error to experience. At last, I have stopped checking to find out how the majority garden and have chosen to go with my gut. I have surely turned enough soil and pulled enough weeds to just get stuck in without over thinking? One thing is for sure, as I've got older I've got more ruthless. If a plant doesn't thrive after a few years of mollycoddling, I get rid of it. Life is too short and with so many other wonderful plants on offer it's far more exciting to move on. Don't fuss, don't panic – it's your garden so you can do what the hell you like. That, of course, comes with the caveat that you must be considerate to those that share your garden – by that I don't mean family but more the wildlife, birds and insects.

Lately, I have definitely decided that it is down to me how I am perceived in the future. There are two options: the first is to retreat to a flower bed with my trowel and be known as the eccentric gardening lady who once wrote for magazines. I have visions of myself as an old lady who lives in a house so clad in climbers and wall shrubs that no one can see in or out and I can dress (or not dress!) without a care in the world. Or, I could continue to keep up with the pace of change in horticulture and remain on my game and acceptably well pruned! If I'm honest both are equally tempting. The one certainty is that I am determined to carry on communicating with fellow gardeners. This might be just over the garden hedge or at a conference – both hold equal value to me. I didn't initially come to gardening to share my experiences with others – I was quite happy to just potter with plants in my own little world. This need to share the passion for plants has only happened because I dared to say yes to nearly every opportunity that has come my way. Confidence was gained, my enthusiasm and often my naivety has served me well and given me some wonderful stories to tell. Thanks to my communications with other gardeners, I am now often described as an 'author', 'lecturer' or 'writer'. I have never quite got used to these descriptions; I'd far rather be known as a 'gardener'.

Ultimately, I was drawn to being a gardener as I had hoped for a quiet, creative life. I'd have done my best at school to avoid unnecessary contact with humans, but this career has made me engage and love people as much as plants which has been very unexpected. Thanks to my career choice I have found my people. When I first considered gardening as a career, all those years ago, it was so frowned upon. Horticulture has since become the thing to embrace whoever you are and however tiny your plot, which is just simply wonderful. I marvel and delight at all the millions of new gardeners and the rampant activity on social media about the subject. I'm eager to shout out very loudly 'Why has it taken you all so long? Welcome to my world.'

With so many new gardeners on the scene you'd have thought that us veterans would be living in fear for our jobs and ready to fend off the new crop with our garden forks, but not a bit of it. How tragic it would be if there weren't new gardeners and enthusiasts following us along the gardening path with pockets full of dreams and new ideas. The sheer joy it brings me when younger adults visit the garden is just wonderful, as I was like them once. Gardening has a future and I like to think that I've done my bit to encourage others to dig in and take part.

Not being one to mislead people, I should say that gardening does come with its stresses and challenges, so don't be fooled into thinking it's all plain sailing. I've outlined a few of them in this book! There is no career where stumbling blocks, deadlines and disasters can be avoided completely, so if you thought gardening was simply about floating around a garden deadheading with a trug romantically hanging from your arm then you might be in for a shock. The only one thing that I can promise you is that plants don't talk back at you – although with the pace of change, anything is possible!

So, what next for me? The priority is to remain physically fit. How frustrating to at last feel you know what you are doing in a garden but not be able to do anything about it. I recently cut down a large shrub and it seemed far more of an event than it used to. Crouching in a packed border with a saw (a blunt saw, I might add) resulted in overheating and a soundtrack of expletives. Once the task had been achieved, I lay on the lawn half undressed to recover but soon realised that the garden was open and visitors might think the gardener had passed out due to over exertion, so I quickly jumped to my feet. I have considered taking up running to prolong my physical health, but the trainers still remain in the cupboard. It seems foolish to use up valuable energy pounding the country lanes when I could be using it to garden. After all, I might get hit by a car, attacked by dogs or get lost (all great excuses). I am convinced that gardening is a terrific way to keep fit and I put this theory to the test a few years ago. My son dared me to run the annual Boxing Day run up and over Croft Ambrey in Herefordshire. Not one to shy away from a challenge, on that occasion I dug out my tracksuit and stood on the starting line with enthusiastic club runners feeling very cold and sick with nerves. I wasn't just in it for the experience, though. Being a competitive sort, I was in it to be placed. I'm not going to say it was easy, especially as I was wearing slightly large football boots rather than trainers so as not to slip, but I came in a very respectable position and shocked the family and myself. Now I have proven my point that gardening is a sport there is no need to attempt any muddy shenanigans again in the future. This was my Shergar moment and there would be no reason to repeat it.

Over time I have learned that one person just can't know everything about gardening and those that claim to are lying or deluded. Anyway, if I am to believe the experiences of others, by the time I have gone through the menopause I'll have forgotten most of the plant names I know anyway! In my opinion, the only sure-fire way of remembering a plant name is to either buy it or propagate it. Spending either money or time on a plant is the only way to sear it into your memory.

So, looking back now, would I change my career choice? I think you will have guessed the answer: absolutely not. Gardening is who I am and what I do, and retirement is not something that is even in my vocabulary. This is partly because most gardeners haven't amassed enough money to retire but also because I wouldn't be able to give up. This last chapter is being written on a summer's day in the garden. On the table I have a vase of *Alchemilla mollis* coupled with geraniums and the birds are filling the air with song. I can smell the scent of the nemesia from the pots that are nearby and occasionally a petal will drop from a nearby rose. There is so much inspiration around me, and so much calm. I might sound a little sentimental, but what would life be without these simple pleasures? The thought that some people live without even noticing these details is beyond comprehension to me. A life without gardening, music and a little humour wouldn't be much of a life at all.

I wanted to write this book to chart the journey of a girl who far from sparkled at school and started her career right at the bottom. My aim was to prove that we all have a gardener within us and that anyone and everyone should give it a go. There is happiness and adventure to be found in a garden – so why don't you come and join me?